AIRPORTS UK

Peter Crook is a senior captain with Genair, Britain's fastest-growing commuter airline. He flies mainly the Shorts SD 330/360, an aircraft ideally suited to commuter traffic, where flying time between landings can be as little as twenty minutes. This traffic intensity ensures that a pilot builds up a detailed knowledge of many of the airports in the UK and quickly learns of the local difficulties that may be encountered. Captain Crook writes about most of the airports in this book from the pilot's viewpoint, and also contributes a valuable introduction which explains basic airfield design, and the various procedures which help a pilot to his destination.

Airfield design

The predominant feature affecting airfield location and runway construction is the prevailing wind direction. An aircraft taking off into wind will be airborne with the shortest ground roll; similarly, after take off it will enjoy the best climb gradient to clear obstacles. On landing into wind the ground speed will be minimised as will roll distance. Formerly, when flying-boats were the rage, one could almost guarantee surface operation into wind. Also early land-based aircraft operating from grass fields could face into wind easily. However, modern passenger aircraft are heavier and require long straight runways on which to operate. It follows that these runways need to face into the prevailing wind which is often from the west or '270°'. Runways are given references based on the direction they face: thus one with a heading of 270° may be called 27/09 (the 09 end being used for reciprocal direction traffic, on heading 090°). When there is a strong cross-wind on the main runway, a shorter one (for example 22/04) may sometimes be used. On a typical airfield the wind strength and direction is shown by the windsock and is accurately measured by the use of an anemometer. The Air Traffic Control (ATC) Local Controller passes this and other precise airfield information to the pilot using radio telephony (RT). The ATC Local Controller is based in the control tower on the airfield.

As aircraft in circuit fly relatively low, the area surrounding the runways should be free of high obstructions – this being particularly necessary on the runway approach and climb-out path. Modern commuter aircraft enjoy Schedule A performance, which means that they can function in complete safety with one engine inoperative. An airfield with no high obstacles enables the pilot to operate to Schedule A at higher all-up weights, permitting the carriage of more passengers and reserve fuel.

The typical aerodrome shape has evolved. In many instances the runways were put down during the Second World War for heavy bombers. Their critical take-off weights necessitated the construction of a third runway to guarantee into-wind lift-off. Approach lighting comprising a centre line with cross bars completes the basic picture. The runway lights are unidirectional, being visible only from the approach path.

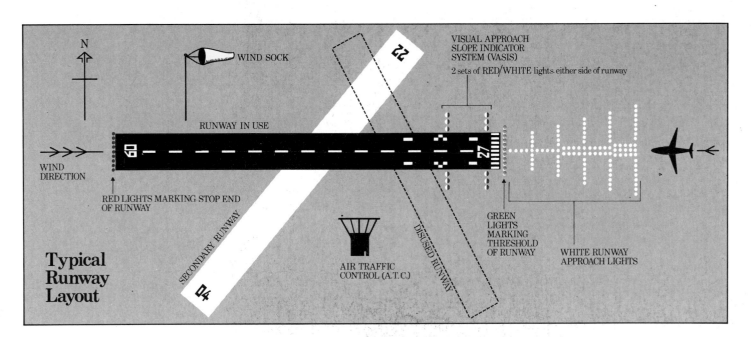

Typical Runway Layout

En route in a Shorts SD 330

On climb out from the typical airfield the usual altitude for the commuter aircraft would be between 4,000 and 10,000 feet. At height all aircraft must have the standard pressure setting of 1013.2 millibars on their altimeters. At these flight levels aircraft heading between north and east always fly with odd thousands of feet indicated on their altimeters, while those heading between south and west have even thousands of feet shown. Thus 1,000 feet separation can be guaranteed for opposing traffic. For the same reason this 'quadrantal rule' requires aircraft heading between east and south to fly at odd thousands of feet plus 500 feet; and between west and north at even thousands plus 500 feet. At lower altitudes the altimeters are set on QNH to assist in terrain avoidance. In circuit they are set on QFE which will indicate aircraft height above touchdown.

After levelling off, *en route* navigation on airways is usually by Voice Omni Range (VOR) beacons with Distance Measuring Equipment (DME) which give the pilot a visual display of range and bearing to a fixed point; thus he can fix his position readily. The DME tells him the number of miles to run, the speed over the ground, and the time to run to the beacon. Each beacon is coded so that the pilot can tune and identify it accurately.

If VORs are not available navigation may be carried out with the assistance of Non-Directional Beacons (NDBs). These give only a relative bearing: one still has to work out drift and distance to run. Two NDBs are needed for an instant fix. Extra navigational assistance is often available from civilian or RAF radar units *en route*, though their main service to pilots is in maintaining adequate separation from other aircraft. Some radar units, particularly in controlled airspace have Secondary Surveillance Radar (SSR) – a derivative of the wartime Identification Friend or Foe (IFF) – which displays aircraft heights and identification on the ground radar returns. Finally, the Flight Information Service (FIS) provides useful in-flight information including news of the weather and airfields. The silicon chip has increased the speed and accuracy of modern 'navaids' and radar as well as their reliability. New aircraft radars are able to depict poor weather and may be used in the mapping mode for navigation.

Before approaching a destination airfield, one must establish that the weather is within limits for a safe approach. On minor airfields ATC relays these details. For larger airports there is an Automated Terminal Information Service (ATIS) which transmits up-to-date weather and airfield information, often on a local tower or VOR frequency. The current weather is allocated an alphabetic code which is altered when the conditions change. Some modern aircraft have radar capable of projecting destination weather on the aircraft radar screen.

The Visual Join

Assuming that destination met (meteorological) conditions are suitable, ATC may clear the incoming aircraft for a visual join to land. Visual assistance is available for such an approach in the form of centre-line lighting, typically a centre line and five cross bars, to give azimuth (heading) guidance, as well as a useful perspective view of the approach. To designate descent path, Visual Approach Slope Indicators (VASIs), located on either side of the runway, comprise two sets of lights on either side of the touchdown point. These show all-red when the pilot is too low, all-white when he is too high, and red/white when he is on the correct glidepath. Alternatively there may be Precision Approach Path Indicators (PAPIs), which comprise four lights in a row, of which the majority appear red if the approach is too low; if too high most of them are white; two reds with two whites indicates the correct glideslope. PAPIs give more precise visual approach guidance than VASIs.

Civilian airfields usually have an omni-directional green light

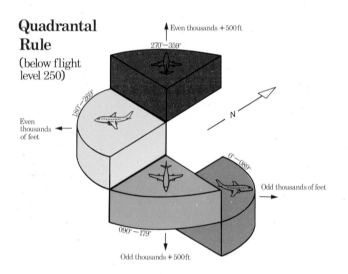

Quadrantal Rule

(below flight level 250)

Even thousands + 500 ft
270°–359°

180°–269°
Even thousands of feet

N

0°–089°
Odd thousands of feet

090°–179°

Odd thousands + 500 ft

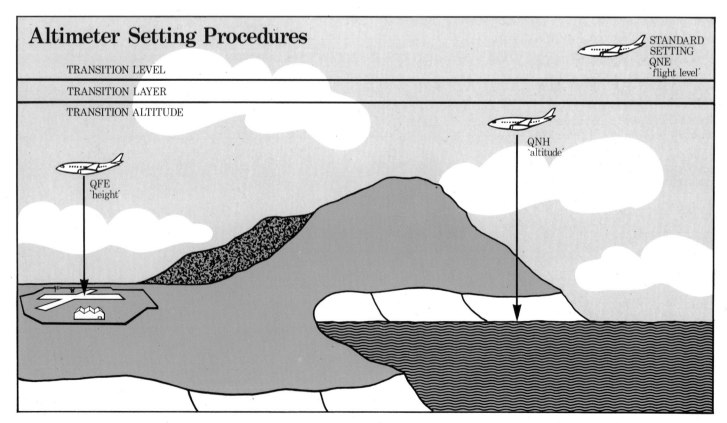

Altimeter Setting Procedures

STANDARD SETTING QNE 'flight level'

TRANSITION LEVEL

TRANSITION LAYER

TRANSITION ALTITUDE

QNH 'altitude'

QFE 'height'

beacon located on the field which flashes identification letters in morse code. Service airfields have red flashing beacons.

The Instrument Join
The cloudbase may be too low to permit visual contact with the airfield. In Instrument Met Conditions (IMC) the pilot locates the centre line using his instruments. He is helped in this by the NDB located four miles or so from the airfield. At the NDB a number of aircraft may hold, flying in a race-track pattern, in the stack at different levels. When cleared by ATC they shuttle down the stack until it is their turn to begin an approach, leaving the NDB at a precise height on track for the airfield. By using a stopwatch, and backtracking from the NDB, the pilot may descend to a 400-foot cloudbase to become visual to land. When there is high-density traffic, ATC may use the stack to space out arrivals. Most airfields are now equipped with NDBs for IMC approaches.

ILS Procedures
If the cloudbase is lower than 400 feet, pilots are not allowed to make an approach using NDB tracking alone – more sophisticated equipment is needed to indicate the runway centre line *and* glidepath. To this end the Instrument Landing System (ILS), located at the airfield, sends localiser and glidepath signals to the aircraft whose instrumentation informs the pilot of position relative to the runway centre line and ideal descent path. Outbound from the NDB, the aircraft flies a procedural turn and homes to the centre line and glidepath. In the 'alternate procedure', the aircraft extends in the NDB hold arriving automatically on the correct inbound heading for the centre line and glidepath. During the approach the Locater Outer Marker (LOM) provides the fix for timing. Often this may be supported by a DME located on the threshold indicating miles to the runway. The incoming aircraft may now descend to a 200-foot cloudbreak. The radar altimeter will indicate when Decision Height is being approached. If the landing cannot be assured the aircraft will go round again from the Missed Approach Point (MAP).

Airfield Radar
If the destination airport is fortunate enough to have its own radar, the radar controller can identify inbound aircraft as traces on his cathode-ray tube and place these aircraft on such a heading that they will intercept the ILS and turn on to the localiser ready to descend on glidepath in due course. If the NDB fails, the Surveillance Radar Approach (SRA) Controller may talk the aircraft down in weather minimum similar to that of

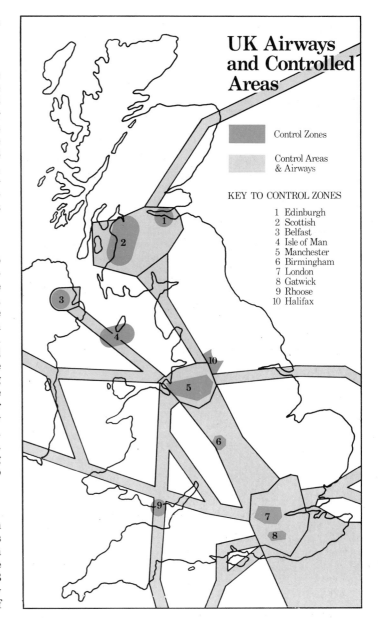

UK Airways and Controlled Areas

Control Zones

Control Areas & Airways

KEY TO CONTROL ZONES
1 Edinburgh
2 Scottish
3 Belfast
4 Isle of Man
5 Manchester
6 Birmingham
7 London
8 Gatwick
9 Rhoose
10 Halifax

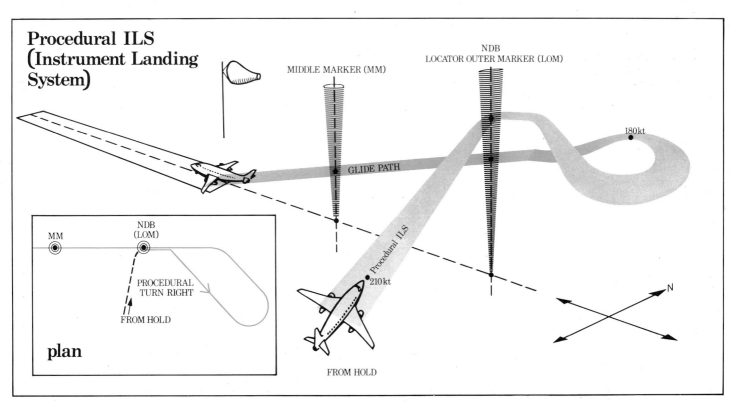

Procedural ILS (Instrument Landing System)

MIDDLE MARKER (MM)

NDB
LOCATOR OUTER MARKER (LOM)

180kt

GLIDE PATH

Procedural ILS

210kt

FROM HOLD

plan

MM

NDB (LOM)

PROCEDURAL TURN RIGHT

FROM HOLD

N

Above: *Heathrow Ground Control: the screen shows the radar scan of the photograph* below; right: *final approach at Heathrow showing runway lights on left.* Opposite page: *the new ground radar installation at Heathrow by Terminal 1 car park.*

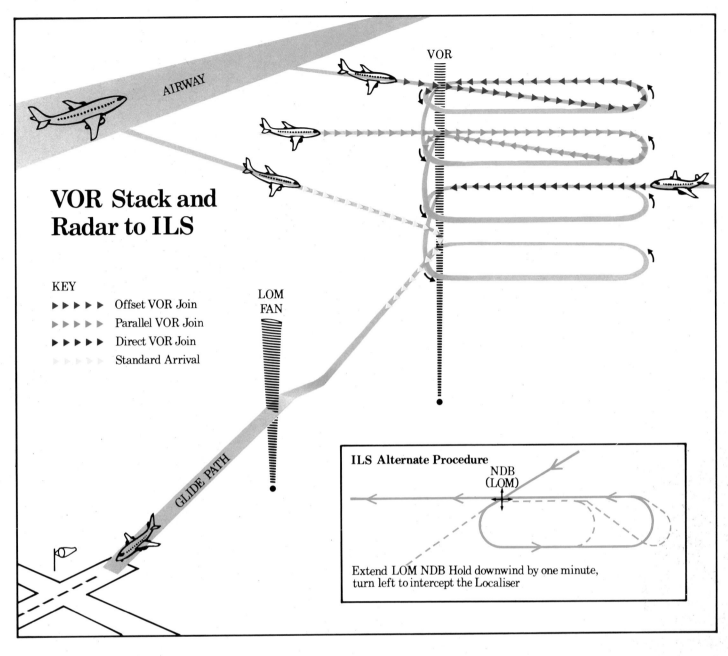

VOR Stack and Radar to ILS

KEY

▶ ▶ ▶ ▶ Offset VOR Join

▶ ▶ ▶ ▶ Parallel VOR Join

▶ ▶ ▶ ▶ Direct VOR Join

▷ ▷ ▷ ▷ Standard Arrival

ILS Alternate Procedure

Extend LOM NDB Hold downwind by one minute, turn left to intercept the Localiser

NDB approach. If the ILS fails and the airfield possesses a Precision Approach Radar (PAR), its controller can fix the aircraft in plan *and* elevation and talk it down to minima similar to that of the ILS. However, radar 'talk down' is expensive in manpower and is usually maintained as a back-up service to inbound ILS traffic.

Many modern aircraft use the auto-pilot in the ILS mode to complete an auto-ILS, leaving the pilot to carry out the landing itself. The latest technology on the ground and in the air can be used to operate the throttles on an auto-coupled ILS approach mode for blind landings as well; bearing in mind the latest technological advances, passenger aircraft may soon operate in complete safety without a pilot at the helm!

Conclusions

From this it can be seen that one airfield may resemble another for both visual and instrument operations. Standardisation in airfield design is a good thing in the interests of flight safety and is extended to *en route* operations for the same reason. As technology advances, pilots are able to rely even more on the modern navigational aids and flight instruments. This reduces the workload and thus improves flight safety.

All this has a significant bearing on commuter-style aircraft operations within the UK. These aircraft make many more take-offs and landings in the course of the year than do their long-haul brethren. Since these are very critical phases in aircraft operation, it is imperative that smaller aircraft enjoy every

modern benefit.

There are two main criteria which ensure the success of commuter-style operations. First and foremost the flight must be safe. The attentions of the Civil Aviation Authority (CAA), allied with the high level of flying and engineering expertise available, combine to create the enviable flight safety record enjoyed in Britain today.

Secondly, there is fierce competition for passenger traffic. Only by strict adherence to schedule times can vital connections be made. Delays due to adverse weather or ATC holds must be minimised. Strenuous efforts are made to speed aircraft movements and to expedite passenger-handling.

Above: *sophisticated snow-clearance machinery ensures that Britain's airports remain open even through the fiercest winter weather*. Opposite left: *over-flying Edinburgh – the runway pattern is shown by standing water reflecting the sunlight.* Opposite right: *freight operations are an important contribution to an airport's finances: here a jumbo with front-loading facilities is being serviced.*

Above: *a Pathfinder foam truck at Manchester. Fire-fighting vehicles can cost as much as £250,000. Below: a Shorts SD 330 operated by Genair. It seats thirty passengers and is powered by* Pratt & Whitney *turboprops, giving maximum speed of 227 mph (365 km/hr) and range of 506 miles (804 km). Opposite: the cockpit controls of a SD 330 – an excellent ergonomic layout.*

In the dialogue below, typical of that which would take place on a flight between Norwich and London, the words spoken by the Captain appear in roman type, those of Air Traffic Control in italic.

Good morning Norwich Tower. EN 103 request start clearance for London Heathrow.

EN 103 clear start. Outside air temperature + 4.

Roger. EN 103 clear start.

....

EN 103 Request taxi.

EN 103. Clear taxi. Runway 27. QNH 1027 QFE 1024. Surface wind 270°/15 knots.

Roger. EN 103. Taxi 27. 1027. 1024.

....

EN 103. Request airways clearance.

EN 103. Roger. London clears EN 103 to join controlled airspace at Brookmans Park. Flight level 80. Squawk 6442. Frequency 125.8.

EN 103 is cleared to join controlled airspace at BPK. Flight level 80. Squawk 6442 on 125.8

EN 103. Readback correct. Call 119.35 for take-off.

EN 103. Roger 119.35.

....

Approach – this is EN 103 at Marshalling Point 27. Ready for take-off.

EN 103. Clear line-up and take-off. Surface wind 270/15.

EN 103 cleared take-off.

....

EN 103 cleared to QSY Honington. Frequency 129.05. Radar hand over.

EN 103 to Honington 129.05. Good day. Honington, this is EN 103 on radar handover from Norwich. Good morning.

EN 103. This is Honington. Good morning. You are identified ten miles south-west of Norwich. Advise reaching flight level 80.

EN 103. Wilco.

....

Honington. EN 103. Flight level 80.

EN 103. Roger. Maintain.

....

EN 103. You are reaching the edge of my radar cover. Are you identified by London?

Honington. EN 103. Affirmative. QSY London. Good day.

EN 103. Good day.

....

London. This is EN 103. Good morning.

EN 103. Good morning. Maintain flight level 80. Route Barkway, Lambourne, London Heathrow. Landing 28L.

Roger. Maintain flight level 80. Route Barkway, Lambourne, Heathrow. Landing 28L.

....

EN 103. Route direct Lambourne. Descend to flight level 70.

EN 103. Direct Lambourne. Descend flight level 70.

....

EN 103. I see you approaching Lambourne. Call leaving Lambourne on 270°.

EN 103. To call leaving Lambourne on 270°. Wilco.

....

EN 103. Leaving Lambourne on 270°.

EN 103. Roger. Call London on 120.4.

EN 103. 120.4. Good day.

....

London. EN 103. Good morning. Shorts SD 230 with 'Echo' (ATIS).

EN 103. Good morning. Descend to 4,000 feet and turn left onto 130°. You are number six for 28L.

EN 103. Descend to 4,000 feet and turn left onto 130°. Wilco.

....

EN 103. Continue descent to 3,000 feet. Turn right onto 180°. Call Radar on 119.2.

Roger. EN 103 descend to 3,000 feet. Turn right onto 180°. To radar on 119.2.

....

Radar, this is EN 103. Good morning.

EN 103. Good morning. Turn further right onto 250. Intercept ILS. Call localiser established 28L.

EN 103. Roger 250°. To call established 28L.

....

EN 103. Established 28L.

EN 103. Roger. Cleared. Descend with ILS 28L. Maintain 175 knots to outer marker. QFE 28L 1020.

EN 103. Roger. Cleared ILS 28L. To maintain 175 knots to outer marker. QFE 1020.

....

EN 103. Outer marker inbound.

EN 103. Continue. Call Tower on 118.7. Good day.

EN 103. Call Tower 118.7. Good day.

....

Tower. Good morning. EN 103.

EN 103. Roger. Continue approach 28L. Number 2.

EN 103. Continue approach 28L.

....

EN 103. Clear land 28L.

EN 103. Clear land 28L.

....

EN 103. Clear right first available. When clear call ground 121.9.

EN 103. First right. Ground 121.9.

....

Ground. EN 103.

EN 103. Good morning. Right on inner to Delta 60.

EN 103. Right inner Delta 60. Wilco.

Ground this is EN 103. Request start for Norwich. We have 'Golf'.

EN 103. Good afternoon. Clear start. Clacton one golf. Squawk 6437.

EN 103. Roger. Clear start. CIG squawk 6437. QSY 121.7. Good day.

....

EN 103. Request taxi. Delta 60.

EN 103. Clear taxi. Turn to face north. Follow the Sabena for hold 28R.

EN 103. Roger clear taxi. North to follow Sabena for hold 28R.

....

EN 103. Call Tower 118.5.

EN 103. Tower 118.5. Good day.

....

Tower. EN 103. Good afternoon.

Good afternoon EN 103. Hold at marshalling point.

EN 103. Holding.

....

EN 103. Clear take-off.

EN 103. Cleared take-off.

....

EN 103. Turn right for Burnham. Call radar 125.8. Good day.

EN 103. Good day.

....

Twin Otter 310. Aurigny Air Services.　　Douglas DC 8–54F. Air Canada.　　Caravelle 10B. Sterling Airways.　　Boeing 747. Pakistan International Airl

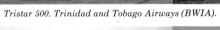

Tristar 500. Trinidad and Tobago Airways (BWIA).　　Douglas DC 10–30. Iberia.　　Douglas DC 10–40. Malaysian Airline System.　　Douglas DC 8–63. Canadian Pacific/Air

Fokker F27 Friendship. Manx Airlines.　　Boeing 747. Wardair Canada Ltd.　　Boeing 737–204. Britannia Airways Ltd.　　Boeing 727. Dan-Air London Ltd.

Tristar 500. The Royal Jordanian Airline.　　Douglas DC 10–30CF. World Airways.　　Boeing 737–205. Braathens SAFE.　　Boeing 747–230B. British Caledonian.

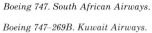

Boeing 747. South African Airways.　　Douglas DC 8–62. Swissair.　　Tupolev Tu–154B. Aeroflot.　　Boeing 737. Maersk Air.

Boeing 747–269B. Kuwait Airways.　　Boeing 707–3B4C. Middle East Airlines.　　Boeing 707–3F9C. Nigeria Airways.　　Douglas DC 10–30. Viasa.

Boeing 737–236. British airtours Ltd.　　Boeing 727–200. Condor Flugdienst.　　Fokker F27 Friendship Mk 200. British Midland.　　Fokker F28/4000 Fellowship. Air France (Air Alsace).

Boeing 747–246F. Japan Air Lines.

AS–332L Super Puma. Bristow Helicopters Ltd.

D.H.C. 7–110 Dash Seven (STOL). Brymon Aviation Ltd.

AIRCRAFT AND LIVERIES

International Civil Aircraft Markings (abbreviated list)

A2 – Botswana
A6 – United Arab Emirates
A7 – Qatar
A9C – Bahrain
A40 – Oman
AP – Pakistan
B – China/Taiwan
C – Canada
CC – Chile
CCCP – Soviet Union
CN – Morocco
CP – Bolivia
CS – Portugal
CX – Uruguay
D – West Germany
DDR – East Germany
EC – Spain
EI – Republic of Ireland
EJ – Republic of Ireland
EL – Liberia
EP – Iran
ET – Ethiopia
F – France
G – United Kingdom
HA – Hungary
HB – Switzerland
HC – Ecuador
HI – Dominican Republic
HK – Colombia

HR – Honduras
HS – Thailand
HZ – Saudi Arabia
I – Italy
JA – Japan
JY – Jordan
LN – Norway
LQ – Argentina
LV – Argentina
LX – Luxembourg
LZ – Bulgaria
N – U.S.A.
OB – Peru
OD – Lebanon
OE – Austria
OH – Finland
OK – Czechoslovakia
OO – Belgium
OY – Denmark
PH – Netherlands
PK – Indonesia
PP – Brazil
PT – Brazil
RP – Philippine Republic
S2 – Bangladesh
S7 – Seychelles
SE – Sweden
SP – Poland
ST – Sudan

SU – Egypt
SX – Greece
TC – Turkey
TF – Iceland
TG – Guatemala
TI – Costa Rica
TJ – Cameroon
TS – Tunisia
TY – Benin
TZ – Mali
VH – Australia
VP–W – Zimbabwe
VP–Y – Zimbabwe
VR–H – Hong Kong
VT – India
XA – Mexico
XB – Mexico
XC – Mexico
XY – Burma
XZ – Burma
YI – Iraq
YK – Syria
YR – Romania
YU – Yugoslavia
YV – Venezuela
ZA – Albania
ZK – New Zealand
ZL – New Zealand
ZM – New Zealand

ZP – Paraguay
ZS – South Africa
ZT – South Africa
ZU – South Africa
4R – Sri Lanka
4W – Yemen
4X – Israel
5A – Libya
5B – Cyprus
5H – Tanzania
5N – Nigeria
5T – Mauritania
5X – Uganda
5Y – Kenya
6Y – Jamaica
7O – Yemen
7Q – Malawi
7T – Algeria
8R – Guyana
9G – Ghana
9H – Malta
9J – Zambia
9K – Kuwait
9L – Sierra Leone
9M – Malaysia
9N – Nepal
9Q – Zaire
9V – Singapore
9Y – Trinidad & Tobago

· Shorts SD 330. Loganair Ltd.

Shorts SD 360. Air Ecosse (Datapost).

BAe/Aerospatiale Concorde. British Airways.

HPR-7 Herald 213. Air UK Ltd.

Lockheed L–100 Hercules. Alaska International Air.

BAe 146. Dan-Air London Ltd.

A 310 Airbus. Lufthansa.

Tristar L10–11. Trans World Airlines.

ABERDEEN

IATA Code: ABZ. **ICAO Code:** EGPD.

Area: 474 acres.

Elevation: 235 feet.

Site: 5 nm NW of city.

Runway: 17/35.   1,829 × 46 metres (6,002 × 150 feet) – asphalt/concrete.

Landing category: ICAO CAT I.

Apron: Ten nose-in aircraft stands.

Aberdeen Tower: 118.1 MHz.

Aberdeen Approach: 120.4 MHz (fixed wing).
                       121.25 MHz (helicopters).

Traffic 1981–82
Terminal passengers: Fixed wing 1,139,500. Helicopters 501,100.
Commercial movements: Fixed wing 41,300. Helicopters 38,400.

Freight: 7,700 tonnes.

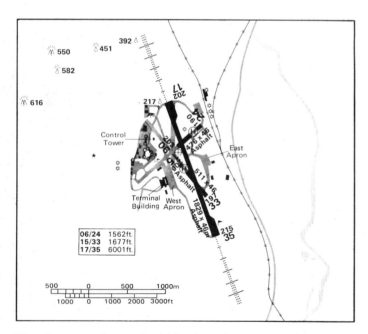

The phenomenal growth of Aberdeen Airport over the last ten years is unparalleled in Britain. In 1981–82 ten times as many people used it as in 1970–71. The cause of this growth has been the development of the offshore oilfields in the North Sea.

One of the great pioneers of Scottish aviation, Eric Gandar Dower, is credited with founding the airport. In March 1931 he landed his Blackburn Bluebird in a rough meadow at Dyce, the local population flocking from their crofts to see the amazing machine. Dower decided that the idea of an airport at Aberdeen was sound commercially and set about levelling the ground. He also began to build up his own airline – Aberdeen Airways – which began its service to Glasgow in September 1934. Further scheduled flights to Orkney and Shetland were established later.

During the Second World War Dyce airfield was requisitioned and served as an important base for Fighter and Coastal Commands who laid down three concrete runways. After the war, the resident airline (by then known as Allied Airways) was wound up and it was left to BEA to begin an Aberdeen–London

service in 1946. A year later the first helicopter used the airport, carrying mail for the GPO. The runways built for the RAF were not found to be suitable for airliners then coming into service and so the present runway was constructed, 6,000 feet in length. The somewhat primitive terminal was situated by the railway on the eastern boundary.

The first expansion of the airport, stimulated by the oil boom, was begun during the time that Aberdeen was administered by the CAA. This work became the responsibility of BAA when they took over on 1 January 1975. The new terminal and apron were built on the opposite (south-western) side of the airport and became operational on 21 June 1977. Special regard was paid to future needs for expansion in the new buildings, and in fact it has become necessary to enlarge many of the facilities since then. After Heathrow, Aberdeen must be Britain's most exciting airport for aviation enthusiasts. In addition to scheduled flights to all parts of the UK and the Continent there is constant activity as helicopters and executive aircraft arrive and depart with oilfield cargoes and personnel. In terms of aircraft movement it is our second busiest airport.

Approaching the airfield from the south, one is conscious that Aberdeen is sometimes prone to sudden weather deterioration. Situated close to the east coast, it is subject to the Haar, a fast-moving and unpredictable sea-fog. Therefore before committing oneself to descent it is always a good idea to tune in to Volmet North on 126.6 for the latest Aberdeen weather. In case this is not hopeful, the same channel includes local diversions such as Edinburgh and Glasgow. The inbound ATC flight-plan nomi-nates diversions should this be necessary. Another factor relevant to operations at Aberdeen is the variety of different types and sizes of aircraft – single and multi-engined, fixed wing and rotary. Again the inbound filed flight-plan is useful to ATC controllers, as aircraft type is specified together with speed, inbound flight level, and flight path.

There is a local coded VOR/DME ADN 114.3 to help navigation and provide ETAs. When the beacon is selected, one can identify it by morse code on the radio. In this case: ·— —·· —· (ADN).

Aberdeen has its own airfield radar which ranges far out to sea to identify and process traffic. Once airfield information is passed, the aircraft is usually fed by radar control into the ILS for RW17.

After landing, first impressions are of a very high-density helicopter environment as choppers constantly shuttle to and from the offshore oil rigs. The complex network of taxiways often carries several helicopters trundling between dispersals and runways.

Passenger handling is usually efficient and well co-ordinated, and the terminal, to the west of the airport, is modern and comfortable.

Departures are clean and simple. Perhaps the high-density air traffic breeds controllers who are specially responsive and helpful.

Opposite page: *Aberdeen is a popular destination for air taxis.*
Above: *industry has quickly surrounded the airport at Dyce.* Left:
*Allied Airways were founded by Gandar Dower and operated
services to Orkney, Shetland and Glasgow from 1935 using Dragon
Rapides.* Below: *a modern rapid intervention fire-fighting vehicle
with a British Airways Chinook helicopter.*

Above: *Gandar Dower's Aberdeen Airways was the first company to operate out of Dyce. Their service to Orkney began in May 1934.* Below: *oil companies use helicopters at Aberdeen to ferry personnel to their rigs offshore. These are Sikorsky S76s.* Right: *two De Havilland Dash 7s are based at Aberdeen for charter work. Operated by Brymon, they have STOL (short take-off and landing) performance, being able to use a strip only 2,000 feet (610 metres) long, carrying fifty passengers.* Below right: *a busy February morning at Aberdeen. SAS use DC 9s for their flights to Oslo, Stavanger and Copenhagen.*

BELFAST
ALDERGROVE

IATA Code: BFS. **ICAO Code:** EGAA.

Area: 693 acres.

Elevation: 267 feet.

Site: 11.5 nm NW of Belfast.

Runways: 08/26.   2,777 × 45 metres (9,111 × 148 feet) – asphalt.
17/35.   1,890 × 46 metres (6,200 × 150 feet) – asphalt.

Landing category ICAO: Category III (a).

Apron: One traffic pier, seven gates, thirteen aircraft stands. Separate general aviation apron.

Belfast Tower: 118.3 MHz.

Belfast Approach: 120.0 MHz.

Traffic 1981–82
Terminal passengers: 1,399,480.
Commercial movements: 67,852.

Freight: 17,738 tonnes.

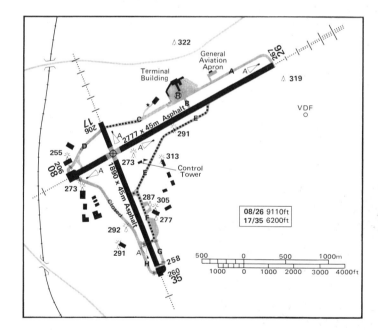

Aldergrove's predecessor was the nearby Nutt's Corner airfield. Two unliveried DC 3s stand on the apron in 1949.

Aldergrove became Northern Ireland's main airport on 26 September 1963. By this time two runways had been constructed: 08/26 (6,005 feet), and 17/35 (6,025 feet). The former was extended to its present length (9,111 feet) in 1973. Further improvements to facilities at the airport raised it to Category III (a) status in 1978.

Today Aldergrove claims to be the sixth busiest airport in the British Isles. It handles an ever-increasing amount of international traffic, and in the summer months is often used by Boeing 747s chartered for transatlantic flights. The British Airways shuttle flights from Heathrow (which now use Boeing 757s) are very popular with business people. It is probably a reflection on the improving situation in the province that flight crews no longer object to staying overnight. A complicated operation from Liverpool ensures that newspaper-readers get their London editions before breakfast-time.

The airport is famous for its hares, and incoming passengers are often amazed as they touch down by the great numbers of the enchanting animal that line the runways to greet them to the Emerald Isle. It is also unique in having a flock of 10,000 golden plovers. If it were not for constant bird-clearing there would be a high accident rate among these rarely encountered birds, as they delight in sitting on the open runways where they have clear views of oncoming predators (but tend to ignore approaching aircraft).

The new self-service refreshment area at Aldergrove. The concourse has recently been refurbished.

Belfast is a city which, over the years, has had a variety of airport sites from which to choose. Newtonards was used for some time in the 1930s (it is now devoted to civilian flying); Sydenham, the harbour airport, was Belfast's airport immediately before the war – it is now used by Shorts and some commuter services; and from 1946 to 1963 the picturesquely named Nutt's Corner was in use.

Aldergrove came into being in 1916 when it was decided to build an airfield here in order that the Handley-Page V/1500 four-engined bombers being built at Harland and Wolff's could be flight-tested and then flown off to the bases where they were to serve. Aldergrove continued as an RAF station after the end of the First World War – remaining a base for bombers (though without hard runways). Vickers Vimys, Handley-Page Hyderabads, and Vickers Virginias were all flown from here. Aldergrove was used briefly by a civil operator in 1933 when Midland and Scottish Air Ferries flew Glasgow–Campbeltown–Belfast.

Above: *British Airways began using the new Boeing 757 on their shuttle services early in 1983 – Rolls Royce economy in an American airframe.* Below: *the spacious layout at Aldergrove. It has been suggested that the American parcels carrier, Federal Express, may use the airport as a base for its European operations. If so, Concorde would be a regular visitor.*

BIRMINGHAM

IATA Code: BHX. **ICAO Code:** EGBB.

Area: 465 acres.

Elevation: 325 feet.

Site: 5.5 nm ESE of city.

Runways: 06/24.   1,315 × 46 metres (4,314 × 150 feet) – tarmac.
15/33.   2,255 × 46 metres (7,400 × 150 feet) – tarmac.

Apron: Present terminal: stands for eleven aircraft.
New terminal: stands for thirteen aircraft.

Birmingham Tower: 118.3 MHz.

Birmingham Approach: 120.5 MHz.

Traffic 1982
Terminal passengers: 1,611,066.
Commercial movements: 63,650.

Freight: 2,211 tonnes.

Spectator facilities (existing terminal): Excellent view of runway from restaurant. Limited space in gallery reached by steps from forecourt.

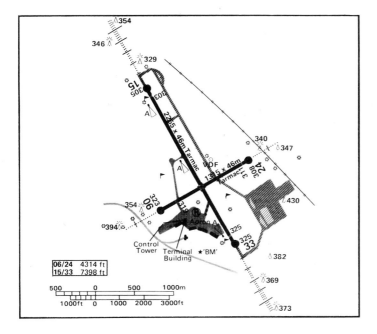

A model of the new layout at Birmingham. The terminal is shown at the bottom of the picture.

History

It seems strange today, in the light of the futuristic terminal buildings to be seen in all corners of the world, that students of architecture should visit Birmingham to view its original terminal, opened in 1939. Yet of all the famous airports designed by the great architects of the 1930s – Berlin, Brussels, Amsterdam, Leipzig, etc. – Birmingham is the sole survivor, providing a unique glimpse of the way a pre-war airport worked. Its most memorable features were the two cantilevered wings that projected from it, intended to give shelter to passengers as they crossed the apron on their way to, or from, their aircraft. The terminal was built of reinforced concrete, and it is a tribute to its designers that it has withstood the passing of the years so effectively. However, there is no arguing that this building, even with its later extensions, has been inadequate for a considerable time, and the opening of the new terminal on the opposite side of

the main runway will be welcomed by all of those who fly from Birmingham, as well as those who work there.

Birmingham's first commercial airport was at Castle Bromwich, and scheduled flights were operated from there up to the opening of the present airport in 1939. However, in 1928 Birmingham City Council had given their approval to the idea of a municipal airport and a site had been chosen – Elmdon. Unfortunately the recession of the 1930s hit the West Midlands particularly badly, and work on the project only progressed in the later years of the decade.

Birmingham (Elmdon) Airport opened on 8 July 1939, a day of drenching rain which caused the planned air display to be cancelled and some of the aircraft to be bogged down (it was a grass airfield). Only a handful of scheduled flights were operated before war broke out two months later and the airport closed down.

During the war Elmdon was used as a Flight Training School and as a testing centre for Stirling and Lancaster bombers, which were built at near-by factories. Two concrete runways were built to facilitate this. Although the airport was relinquished by the RAF in 1946, BEA were slow to resume scheduled flights from Birmingham, their initial service only coming into operation in April 1949. This was a Dakota service linking Manchester with Paris which stopped at Birmingham *en route*. Birmingham has enjoyed a virtually uninterrupted service with Paris ever since.

A slow, steady expansion of services took place over the years up to 1960, when the airport was transferred back to Birmingham City Council from the Ministry of Civil Aviation. During the previous year the main runway had been extended by 800 feet so that it could be used by the Viscount 800s which BEA were beginning to use on flights to continental destinations. On 31 October 1960 a BEA Dakota made the last scheduled flight by this classic type of aircraft from London to Birmingham. The airline made the event a public relations exercise, and several distinguished journalists and broadcasters were on board when the aircraft took off from Heathrow. As it approached Birmingham the weather deteriorated so that ground visibility was almost zero. After circling Birmingham for some time, the captain of the Dakota thought he detected an improvement in conditions and brought the plane down. The Dakota overshot and came to rest with her tail in the air well beyond the end of the runway. Miraculously nobody was hurt.

After a long delay, another extension of the main runway was completed in 1967 when it reached its present length of 7,400 feet. The idea of a new terminal close to the NEC (National Exhibition Centre) was first put forward in 1970 by the Airport Committee of Birmingham City Council, but they were unable to interest the Government in the proposal. The cost at that time was estimated at £3,000,000. By November 1971 this cost had escalated to almost £8,000,000, and although the NEC received Government blessing at the time, the plans for the new terminal were shelved, not to be revived for another eight years, by which time the cost had risen to £29,000,000. Control of Birmingham Airport passed from the City Council to West Midlands County Council in 1974.

Right: *an artist's impression of the new terminal and MAGLEV system at Birmingham.* Below: *the old terminal, showing the two cantilevered 'wings', one of them now covered in.*

The New Terminal

At the time of writing work on the new terminal is reaching its final stages and it should be in operation in 1984. It will virtually double the capacity of the airport to 3,000,000 passengers per year, and many other improvements are being undertaken at the same time.

The site chosen is on the north-east side of the main runway. Birmingham International Station and the NEC are just 600 metres away, and a Space Age transit system – the first of its kind in the world – will link the terminal to the station and the NEC. The new system is called MAGLEV and utilises the principle of magnetic levitation to provide a smooth, quiet ride in cars driven by linear induction motors. No wheels connect the cars with the ground, the only contact being through the electrical pick-up. Two MAGLEV cars will operate on separate tracks, each holding thirty-two passengers and their baggage. It will take ninety seconds for the cars to travel between terminal and station. The success of the system will lead to other airports installing it.

The three-storey terminal building, clad in moulded panels and tinted glass, will contain all the facilities that the traveller expects: buffets, restaurant, duty-free shops, etc. Aerobridges leading from finger-piers will ensure that passengers are protected from the elements as they board, or disembark from, their aircraft.

The apron will provide stands for eight international flights and four domestic ones. New taxiways leading from the terminal will do away with another of Birmingham's traditional problems: the necessity of backtracking down the main runway when arriving from the south-east.

Currently a wide range of domestic and international scheduled services are operated from Birmingham Airport by British Airways, British Midland Airways and other operators. Charter services are a very significant sphere of operation, with numerous operators serving destinations in over twenty countries. The availability of new terminal and aircraft-handling facilities will provide the basis for a significant expansion of services, both in terms of frequency to existing locations and establishing routes to new destinations.

With a geographical location in the heart of England, access for the air traveller could not be easier or more convenient. By car, the new airport is only a few minutes by high standard motorway and dual-carriageway from the M42 and the national motorway network (M6, M1 and M5) which reaches all parts of the country. In addition, the revolutionary MAGLEV shuttle-train system will connect the airport with Birmingham International Railway Station and the National Exhibition Centre. Regular BR Inter-City rail connections are available to all main centres, both to the south and to the north.

This is not an easy airfield to find visually, hence it is usual to ask for radar positioning to ILS on Runway 33. There are also two NBSs: EM and EX. The Honiley VOR/ATIS on 112.9 gives reliable up-to-date cloudbase and visibility readings together with wind velocity. If there is a cross-wind from the direction of the hangars there can be turbulence in the later stages of the approach. This, together with the resultant higher ground speed, may require particularly high levels of concentration to achieve smooth touchdowns. The secondary runway (24/06) is a little short for larger aircraft unless the wind strength is relatively high in that direction. For a cross-wind landing the aircraft may be flown down the slope 'crabbed' into wind, the drift being kicked straight on round-out. Alternatively the wing may be tilted slightly into wind until the later stages. Some aircraft handle best with a combination of the two techniques. If turbulence is momentarily too great, regulations permit an overshoot and second attempt before diversion (always providing that the aircraft has sufficient fuel). After landing, aircraft park in the south-west quadrant, leaving only a short walk for the passengers.

Departures are usually well co-ordinated although the need to backtrack can lead to short delays for take-offs. The new terminal facilities should lead to an increase in density of air traffic.

EDINBURGH

IATA Code: EDI. **ICAO Code:** EGPH.

Area: 901 acres.

Elevation: 135 feet.

Site: 5 nm W of city.

Runways: 07/25. 2,560 × 46 metres (8,399 × 150 feet) – concrete.
08/26. 909 × 46 metres (2,982 × 150 feet) – tarmac.
Used by light aircraft, at most times this strip can be used simultaneously with the main runway.
13/31. 1,829 × 46 metres (6,000 × 150 feet) – tarmac. This was the original runway, but not being aligned into the prevailing wind, it is rarely used.

Apron: Nine stands: three aerobridges.

Edinburgh Tower: 118.7 MHz.

Edinburgh Approach: 121.2 MHz.

Traffic 1981–82
Terminal passengers: 1,201,700.
Commercial movements: 25,600.

Freight: 800 tonnes.

Spectator facilities: The spectator gallery runs along one side of the second floor of the terminal building giving good views of the principal runway.

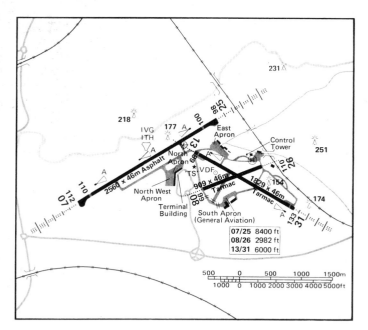

The first airfield was established on the site in 1915, and this became RAF Turnhouse after the end of hostilities in 1918. From 1925 Turnhouse was occupied by the City of Edinburgh Squadron of the Royal Auxiliary Air Force. It was still a grass airfield at this time and in 1928 the Imperial Airways Armstrong Whitworth Argosy *City of Glasgow* landed here at the end of its race with the LNER train hauled by the Pacific locomotive, *Flying Scotsman*. Turnhouse received its first scheduled service in 1935 when North Eastern Airlines operated a route here from Heston via Leeds and Newcastle.

In 1939 paved runways were laid by the RAF for Fighter Command who remained in occupation after the war, even

Disembarking from a BEA DC 3 ('Pionair') at the old Turnhouse Airport. The Dakotas were the workhorses on domestic routes in the decade after the end of the Second World War.

though BEA were allowed to operate services from 1947. The airport was formerly handed over to the Ministry of Civil Aviation in 1960. Even before this date Edinburgh Corporation (who received control of the airport from the Ministry) had carried out improvements. The main runway was lengthened and made stronger and a new terminal building opened in 1956. These facilities were already proving inadequate when the airport again changed hands in 1971, the Scottish Division of the BAA being the new operators. A condition of the airport's transfer to the BAA was a Government grant which covered 75 per cent of the cost of constructing a new runway and terminal complex. The new runway was needed because the existing one was not aligned into the prevailing wind, and strong cross-winds often made landings difficult. This new runway had been in operation for a year when HM The Queen opened the new terminal on 22 May 1977. It is designed to accommodate up to 1,500,000 passengers a year. Since traffic at Edinburgh continues to grow, that figure is now being approached. Fortunately the improvements of the 1970s were designed so that extensions could be made easily. However, one difficulty remains with this airport – its lack of an adequate taxiway means that aircraft have to backtrack along the main runway.

Scheduled flights from Edinburgh are mainly to domestic destinations, the shuttle services offered by British Airways and British Caledonian being particularly popular with travellers catching onward flights from Heathrow.

The usual approach to Edinburgh from the east brings inbound aircraft north of the city and along the Firth of Forth. The radar controller feeds the aircraft on to the ILS/DME and, during an approach to the main runway 25/07, the pilot is often warned of 'wind shear'. The wind from the surrounding high ground bears down on the runway approach and may cause the indicated airspeed to fluctuate. It is possible to gain or lose speed and this should be taken into account, especially in the later stages when speeds are lowest.

After landing, one taxis past huge archimedean-screw water pumps on the edge of the apron to the stand nominated by a flashing light.

The southerly Standard Instrument Departure (SID) requires the flight to pass by Talla VOR 113.8. In order to assess drift at height one should remember that wind direction tends to veer clockwise with increase in height and increase in strength. Hence a light north-westerly breeze at ground level could lead to a strongish northerly wind at height, varying the SID.

Above: *the old airfield at Edinburgh, with its inadequate runways, is shown on the right of this photograph which also features the Firth of Forth (with its two bridges) in the distance. Below; a* *Loganair Twin Otter being re-fuelled at Edinburgh. This rugged aircraft is ideal for the rough landing surfaces sometimes encountered in the Highlands and islands.*

GLASGOW

IATA Code: GLA. **ICAO Code:** EGPF.

Area: 786 acres.

Elevation: 26 feet.

Site: 6 nm W of city.

Runways: 23/05. 2,566 × 46 metres (8,419 × 150 feet) – concrete/asphalt with friction course.
10/28. 1,088 × 46 metres (3,570 × 150 feet) – tarmac. (This used mainly by light aircraft.)

Landing category ICAO: Category III (a).

Apron: Two piers, twenty-eight stands. Twelve stands remote from terminal. Separate helicopter area. Separate executive aircraft apron with stands for up to twenty aircraft.

Glasgow Tower: 118.8 MHz.

Glasgow Approach: 119.1 MHz.

Traffic 1981–82
Terminal passengers: 2,407,300.
Commercial movements: 52,800.

Freight: 12,700 tonnes.

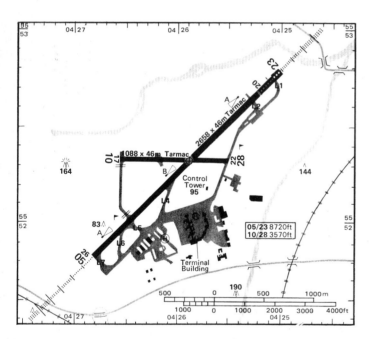

Glasgow is by far the busiest airport operated by BAA's Scottish Division. The city's first airport was situated at Renfrew, but a cramped site surrounded by various obstacles made its development unfeasible, and in 1960 it was decided that Abbotsinch should be adopted as the new Glasgow airport. Abbotsinch was constructed in 1932 as a military airfield and was the headquarters of the local Royal Auxiliary Air Force squadron. In September 1943 it was transferred to the Fleet Air Arm and became HMS *Sanderling*. Subsequently two paved runways were constructed. At this time upwards of 1,000 personnel were stationed at the base. After the war it was used as a maintenance depot for fighters from British, American and Canadian aircraft-carriers. On 31 October 1963 HMS *Sanderling* was decommissioned and the station's crest and bell entrusted to the civil

The terminal building at Glasgow seen from the roof of the Excelsior Hotel. On the right is a Boeing 727 Pax/Freighter of Icelandair who operate scheduled services to Reykjavik.

authority which took over the airfield. The new Glasgow Airport, owned and operated by Glasgow City Corporation, was opened on 27 June 1966 by HM The Queen. Subsequently both runways were improved, the longer one up to Category III (a) standards making Glasgow the first British airport after Heathrow to attain this status. This runway has a sixty by ninety metre area at its north-east end where a Jumbo may turn safely, though Boeing 747s are comparatively rare visitors to Glasgow.

On 1 April 1975 the BAA took over Glasgow Airport from the City Corporation, and since then the number of passengers using the airport has regularly topped 2,250,000. The airport offers all aspects of modern aviation operations from private light aircraft to the large airliner. It is the headquarters of Loganair, the carriers who operate Islanders, Shorts SD 330s, and Twin-Otters to the remote airstrips of the Highlands and Islands. British Airways operate a shuttle service to Heathrow, inaugurated in 1975. There are scheduled flights from Glasgow to more than sixty destinations in Britain and Europe and the airport is busy in the summer with charter flights, some of which take the Scots away for their holidays while others bring in tourists from abroad.

Since its takeover by the BAA there have been many improvements. The terminal has been extended to allow more room for international operations and aerobridges have been installed. Glasgow is an important link in the chain of UK airports and seems certain to continue its expansion in the future.

Approaching from the SE under zone radar, the usual entry to Glasgow is via Talla VOR 113.8 with the Scottish controller. The ATIS can be found on the VOR 113.4 'GOW'; the main runway is 23/05. A visual approach to Runway 23 is very interesting as one runs parallel to the River Clyde on the left where the shipyards provide changing views daily. At night the welding torches make a dramatic scene as the aircraft lets down to land, nearly at sea-level.

An instrument approach to Runway 23 necessitates flying to the NDB 'GLG' located in the hills to the north-east of the airport. If conditions are windy or unstable the effect of these hills is to accentuate the turbulence, hence one avoids instrument approaches if in Visual Met Conditions (VMC). If, on the other hand, there are Instrument Met Conditions (IMC), then the Radar Controller can provide guidance along the Clyde Valley towards the short Runway 28. The aircraft may then land on 28, or circle to approach on 23, leaving the runway via the high-speed turn-off and parking on Stand 15, nose-in to face the BA shuttle pier.

After turn round, the Talla SID (Standard Instrument Departure) is flown. Since the SID routes aircraft over the NDB 'AC' in the hills, an early turn direct to Talla is requested to avoid turbulence and low cloud. The maximum altitude in the zone is 5,500 feet. One has to clear with Scottish ATC before climbing above 5,500 feet to cruise at flight level 75 or 95.

Above: *the terminal and apron (with runway in the background) at Glasgow. Note the airport's proximity to the Motorway (M8).*
Below: *Renfrew Airport about thirty years ago. Again the Dakota is predominant.* Right: *Renfrew photographed on 27 October 1948. The Rapide is being closely guarded.*

Above: *the approach to Glasgow on a wet evening as darkness falls. The river is a tributary of the Clyde on the northern edge of the airport.* Below: *a BEA Heron photographed at Abbotsinch in the early days of the airport.* Right: *British Airways Scottish Division are fighting their way back to profitability with the help of the economical BAe 748, fondly known as 'Budgies'.*

INVERNESS

IATA Code: INV. **ICAO Code:** EGPE.

Area: 395 acres.

Elevation: 31 feet.

Site: 7 nm NE of Inverness at Dalcross.

Runways: 24/06.   1,887 × 48 metres (6,190 × 157 feet).
30/12.   700 × 18 metres (2,296 × 59 feet).

Apron: Three stands self-parking on south apron facing
terminal. Customs area. Six stands on north apron.
Separate helicopter area.

Ground/Approach: 122.6 MHz.

Traffic 1981–82
Terminal passengers: 139,029.
Commercial movements: 11,585.

Freight: 360 tonnes.

The first airfield at Inverness was located at Longman, just half
a mile from the centre of the town. It was from this field that
Captain Fresson flew when he inaugurated the first scheduled
service to the Orkneys for Highland Airways on 8 May 1933. A
year later a Royal Mail contract was awarded to the same
operator. In 1939 Captain Fresson persuaded an Air Ministry
survey team to investigate Dalcross as a possible site for a new,
larger airfield. They found the site to be acceptable and made a
grass airfield there where concrete runways were put down soon
after the outbreak of war in 1939.

After the war both service and civilian traffic operated out of
Dalcross until 1953 when the airport came under the ownership
of the Civil Aviation Authority who have operated it ever since.
Modern terminal facilities (including a bar, cafeteria, bookshop
and bank) cater for domestic and international flights. Inverness
Airport has become a vital link in the transportation scheme for
the Highlands and Islands.

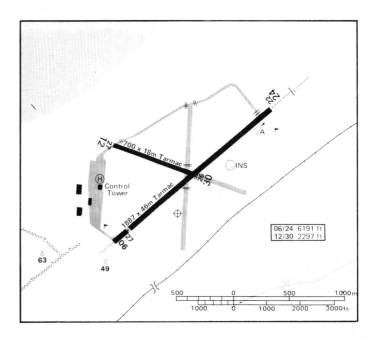

*Inverness is operated by the CAA and its traffic has grown steadily
over the years. Two daily flights link the Highlands with
Heathrow.*

ISLE OF MAN

IATA Code: IOM. **ICAO Code:** EGNS.

Area: 850 acres.

Situation: At Ballasalla, near Castletown.

Elevation: 55 feet.

Runways: 04/22.   1,266 × 46 metres (4,153 × 150 feet) – tarmac.
09/27.   1,753 × 46 metres (5,751 × 150 feet) – tarmac.
18/36.   903 × 27 metres (2,962 × 88 feet) – tarmac.

Apron: Eastern and western aprons. Six self-manœuvring stands. Separate cargo area (Manx Airport Services Ltd.).

Ronaldsway Tower: 118.9 MHz.

Ronaldsway Approach: 120.85 MHz.

Traffic 1982
Terminal passengers: 283,140.
Commercial movements: 9,580.

Freight: 1,533 tonnes.

Spectator facilities: First-floor balcony of terminal building provides good view of apron; also grassed area adjacent to public car park.

The newly-formed Manx Airlines (a division of British Midland) operate Fokker Friendships with appropriate registrations. Here are G-OMAN pictured at Ronaldsway, and G-IOMA (below).

have ensured that the equipment in use at Ronaldsway (including the ILS and Surveillance Radar) is the best available for an airport of this size. The recently formed Manx Airlines are the main operators out of Ronaldsway today: they fly year-round scheduled services to many airports on the mainland (at the time of writing, to Heathrow, Blackpool, Glasgow, Liverpool and Manchester, as well as Dublin and Belfast).

Appropriately, Ronaldsway was a landing-place for the Vikings who used it to supply their stronghold at Castle Rushen. The path from beach to castle was known as 'Ronald's Way'. Later the sheltered beach became Derbyhaven (after the Derby Lords of Man) and was for some time the principal port of the island.

The first airfield on the site became operational in 1934. It was a grass field used by De Havilland Dragons and Fox Moths, and was developed by Isle of Man Air Services who became chief operators. When war broke out in 1939 the RAF used it as a gunnery school but later it was taken over by the Admiralty as a training base for Barracuda torpedo- and dive-bombers of the Fleet Air Arm. It was at this time that the runways were laid down and the hangars and control tower constructed.

In 1946 the airfield was bought by the Manx Government and an Airports Board was set up to administer and develop it. They built the Terminal Building, opened in 1953, and over the years

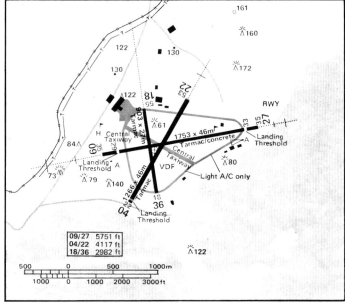

JERSEY

IATA Code: JER. **ICAO Code:** EGJJ.

Area: 332 acres.

Elevation: 276 feet.

Runway: 09/27.   1,706 × 46 metres (5,597 × 150 feet) – asphalt.

Apron: One pier: fourteen nose-in stands. Seven remote stands (on far side of apron from terminal). Separate cargo area and Aurigny Air Services terminal.

Jersey Tower: 119.45 MHz.

Jersey Approach: 120.3 MHz.

Traffic 1981–82
Terminal passengers: 1,348,902.
Commercial movements: 47,624.

Freight: 7,744 tonnes.

Spectator facilities: access is allowed to terminal roof allowing good view of apron, but best view of runway is probably from far side of runway, by lane running past council houses at St Peter's.

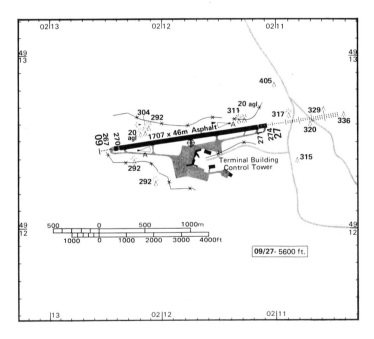

Jersey Airport photographed on a busy Saturday in summer when BIA were still operating. They have since been taken over by Air-UK.

Notwithstanding such difficulties as the tidal conditions, lack of radio and meteorological facilities and passenger-handling accommodation – passenger-processing being carried out in the open air – the services, nevertheless, maintained a high level of regularity and punctuality, thus fostering an increasing interest in the island, in air travel. Twenty thousand passengers were carried in the first year.

Meanwhile, the Jersey Chamber of Commerce had been investigating the possibility of providing a 'land' airport in Jersey and had presented a report to the States of Jersey on the subject. Ground and aerial surveys were undertaken and the present site was identified as being the most suitable.

With the opening of Jersey Airport, it was possible to schedule air services without 'having regard to tidal considerations' and on 10 March 1937 the first air service, operated by Jersey Airways Limited with a De Havilland Express (86) airliner, landed at Jersey Airport.

In April 1937, newspapers were carried to the island by air for the first time and consequently arrived on the same day, having previously been sent by sea and as a result, were normally a day late in arriving. On 1 June 1937 the first air mail service operated. These two events, together with the introduction of regular schedules and new routes, firmly established air travel to and from the island. The air services continued in popularity and on a busy day 600 passengers were handled at the airport.

However, in 1939, the 'clouds of war' were appearing and after the declaration of war, civil aviation flights to and from the island were curtailed. In February 1940, a Fleet Air Arm training squadron was based at Jersey Airport, using Swordfish and Albacore aircraft, but the fortunes of war were seriously to affect the island and eventually Jersey was declared an 'open town'. In June 1940, Jersey Airport came under the control of the German authorities for the duration of the occupation.

On 10 May 1945 airport staff still in the island were recalled to duty to assist the Royal Air Force in restoring the airport to use and on 2 October of the same year the airport was handed over, by the Royal Air Force, to the States of Jersey.

Gradually, the momentum of civil aviation increased and during the years 1946 to 1952, the whole pattern of the island's economy experienced a process of change, brought about, to a great extent, by the increasing popularity of air travel, and in 1952 a tarmac runway was completed, the initial length of which was 4,200 feet. This has, over the years, been lengthened so that it is now 5,597 feet long. At its western (St Ouen's Bay) end is a soft-ground arrester system. This is designed to prevent aircraft overshooting and plunging over the escarpment.

Jersey Airport provides an important link with the mainland and the Continent for the inhabitants of the island and is vital for the continuance of the major industries of the island, that is, finance-centre activities, tourism and agriculture and it is, together with the main seaport of St Helier, one of the two major exit and entry points for passengers and freight.

Prior to the Second World War, several unsuccessful attempts were made to run air services to Jersey. However, in December 1933, a company registered as 'Jersey Airways Limited' commenced scheduled services between the island and the mainland and the first service departed from Jersey to Portsmouth on 18 December 1933, from the 'beach aerodrome' in St Aubins Bay.

The 'beach aerodrome' was situated on a stretch of tidal sand and regular daily schedules were entirely dependent on the state of the tide! The aircraft used were De Havilland Dragons, capable of carrying seven passengers, and in summer the complete fleet of eight aircraft would be used, flying from Portsmouth in loose formation, and parking tail-in to the sea-wall.

Top: *ATC Jersey Tower: note wind speed and direction indicators on the left.* Above: *DH Rapides at Jersey in the late 1940s or early 1950s. BEA called these aircraft 'Islanders'.* Right: *pilots' briefing room. Met information is being plotted in the foreground.* Below right: *the comfortable bar at Jersey Airport which gives an excellent view of the runway.*

During the last three decades the airport has, like most airports throughout the world, been developed and expanded to cater for larger aircraft and the increase in air traffic and now handles some 80,000 aircraft each year, of which over 50,000 are air transport movements.

The Port Authority provides its own technical services for Jersey Airport, that is, air traffic control, telecommunications, navigation aids and meteorological services and is also responsible for the provision of *en-route* services in the Channel Islands Control Zone, the greater part of which is in the French Flight Information Region and it is, therefore, the only organisation in the British Isles, apart from the United Kingdom Civil Aviation Authority, to provide such *en-route* services.

LONDON
GATWICK

IATA Code: LGW. **ICAO Code:** EGKK.

Area: 1,876 acres.

Elevation: 202 feet.

Site: 5 nm S of Redhill.

Runway: 26/08. 3,098 × 46 metres (10,165 × 150 feet) – concrete with friction course.

Apron: Sixty-three stands, twenty-seven of them for wide-bodied aircraft. Eight cargo stands.

Gatwick Tower: 119.45 MHz.

Gatwick Approach: 119.6 MHz.

Gatwick Ground Movement Control: 121.8 MHz.

Traffic 1981–2
Terminal passengers: 11,154,200.
Commercial movements: 132,200.

Freight: 120,300 tonnes.

Spectator facilities: Roof gallery (admission charged) and main restaurants.

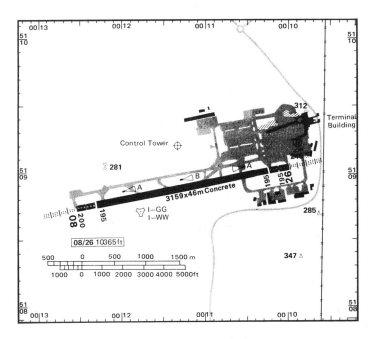

History
The first Gatwick Airport was a grass aerodrome situated at Lowfield Heath, between the main London to Brighton road and the railway to the east. It was a private airfield, opened in 1931, and used mainly by members of the Surrey Aero Club. In 1936 this airfield was substantially expanded and was licensed as 'London South (Gatwick)'. The distinctive circular terminal building of those days, first known as the 'Martello Tower' and later as the 'Beehive', still stands as part of the complex that houses British Airways Helicopter Division – to the south of the modern airport. The Gatwick Airport of the late 1930s was basically a grass airstrip which was perfectly adequate for the commercial planes of that era. Telescopic canvas-covered jetties sheltered passen-

Gatwick from the north, showing the new satellite. Note the proximity of motorway and railway to the terminal.

gers as they walked from the terminal to their aircraft waiting on the apron. A station was specially built to serve the airport, linked to it by tunnel: this made Gatwick the world's first airport to have its own station. The chief disadvantage of Gatwick was that it became waterlogged in wet weather, but even so it was considered worth while to install one of the earliest flying aids here in 1937 – the Lorenz blind-approach system.

During the war Gatwick became an operational base for the RAF who built two steel-reinforced runways, the longest 4,200 feet long. In the 1950s planners realised that it was impossible to rely on just one airport (Heathrow) to serve London and so more than fifty sites for a second airport were investigated. At this time it was intended that this should serve as a diversion airport and as a base for the independent airlines serving London. After considerable opposition from landowners, Gatwick was the site chosen, though the main development was planned for an area away from the old airport, on land occupied previously by Gatwick Racecourse. Thus the present terminal stands where the imposing grandstand once stood. The Brighton road was diverted eastwards away from the new 7,000-foot runway and the old racecourse station was the basis for the one that now links the airport with Central London. The terminal had a single pier

Gatwick is the headquarters of British Caledonian, Britain's largest independent airline. This night shot shows one of their DC 10s.

which led to the apron where there were stands for twenty-one aircraft, eleven of them round the pier itself. HM The Queen opened the new Gatwick on 9 June 1958.

In the 1960s two further piers were constructed and improvements continued throughout the following decade so that Gatwick can now handle all types of aircraft on its 10,000-foot runway. Another important development was the opening of the M23 which gives much-improved access to the capital and to Britain's motorway network.

Gatwick Today

Gatwick has long had the reputation of being one of Europe's most modernistic airports (this perhaps symbolised by its new mushroom-shaped control tower, remote from the terminal buildings). The Satellite-Pier 3 development has also enhanced this reputation. The Satellite, opened in 1983, replaces the original north pier of the terminal which dated from the 1960s. The new pier handles up to 2,400 passengers per hour. It is designed to accept the stretched Jumbos of the future, and has stands for eight wide-bodied aircraft. A hydrant fuel system, also used elsewhere in the airport, reduces clutter on the ground and enables aircraft to refuel quickly and safely. An automated rapid-transit system – the first of its kind at an airport outside the USA – takes passengers to and from the Satellite. Two rubber-tyred vehicles are used, each able to hold up to 100 passengers. As one of these vehicles leaves the main terminal, the other leaves the Satellite. The quarter-mile journey takes less than a minute.

The Satellite itself is a large departure lounge, with duty- and tax-free shops, buffet, bar, etc. From here there is direct access via modern jetties to aircraft.

Gatwick was once famous as a departure point for charter flights. Today it handles more scheduled services (120-plus) than charters, many of the former to long-haul destinations (Hong Kong, Los Angeles, São Paulo, Karachi, etc.). There is also an increasing commuter trade with flights from many of the smaller British airports arriving at Gatwick to connect with intercontinental or European services. A regular helicopter link connects London Gatwick with London Heathrow. The S61, aptly registered G-LINK, flits to and fro to speed the onward traveller. All this, with the ever-growing cargo traffic helps to raise Gatwick up the league table of the world's international airports (at present it is the fourth busiest).

The amazing automated rapid-transit system at Gatwick. It connects the Satellite with the Terminal.

The cargo terminal is on the north-west side of the airport. It has eight aircraft stands, four of them for Boeing 747Fs, and four for other wide-bodies. The spacious layout of the airport allows easy loading and unloading, with trucks able to pull alongside aircraft (even those at the passenger terminal). There are nine transit sheds which give 16,500 square metres of bonded storage. It is planned to double Gatwick's cargo capacity in the next ten years.

London's second airport has only one main runway – 26/08. At busy periods ATC has to be slick to enable aircraft to take off and land expeditiously. There are plans to utilise a smaller subsidiary runway for some commuter operations. Meanwhile inbound aircraft are usually marshalled for Runway 26 on an 'Eastwood' approach. Airfield details are specified by the Mayfield VOR/ATIS 117.9. The Radar Controller positions the aircraft for ILS/DME approaches via NDB 'GE' on 26, 'GY' on 08, and when visual the PAPIs provide very accurate glidepath information. At night on the final approach, there is a brilliantly lit car park at the threshold of Runway 26, and at the far end of the airfield there are two flashing red beacons – very distinctive! After touchdown, a short landing roll permits the aircraft to use the high-speed turn-off to the taxiways. These are centre-lit green. Red stop bars can be illuminated by ground control. Inbound commuter aircraft follow the greens to a pan dedicated to their use.

A first-rate radio network ensures that ground handling is prompt and efficient, both for passengers and aircraft logistics. This is helpful as regulations require an accurate loadsheet to be prepared for every sector. As payload consists of passenger weight, baggage weight, plus fuel weight, only by using accurate passenger and baggage figures can the fuel uplift be ascertained.

Before departure, pre-flight alphabetic data and start-up clearance is available. After start, the aircraft will be directed to an alphabetical runway entry point depending on take-off performance. The Standard Instrument Departure (SID) is designed so that aircraft avoid Heathrow traffic to the north.

Above: *again the rail and road network is well shown in this aerial view of Gatwick. Note the generous car parking, which can still seem inadequate at times.* Below: *a Genair SD 330 and a B-Cal DC 10 photographed together. Although financially independent, the feeder company works in close harmony with the international operator.* Right: *an airport offers the photographer many moments of beauty and grace.*

LONDON HEATHROW

IATA Code: LHR. **ICAO Code:** EGLI.

Area: 2,958 acres.

Elevation: 80 feet.

Site: 12 nm W of Westminster Bridge, London.

Runways: 05/23. 2,357 × 46 metres (7,734 × 150 feet) – concrete. This is the cross-wind runway.
10L/28R. 3,902 × 46 metres (12,802 × 150 feet) – concrete with friction course.
10R/28L. 3,658 × 46 metres (12,000 × 150 feet) – concrete with friction course.
Both main runways have 23-metre (75-feet) paved shoulders along original length and 7.6-metre shoulders along western extensions.

Apron: Total stands 152 (including cargo).

Heathrow Tower: 118.7; 121.9 MHz.

Heathrow Approach: 119.2; 119.5; 120.4; 127.55 MHz.

Traffic 1981–82
Terminal passengers: 26,839,911.
Aircraft movements: 266,483.

Cargo: 450,000 tonnes.

Spectator facilities: Gallery on roof of arrivals hall. Admission charge. Shop and refreshment room.

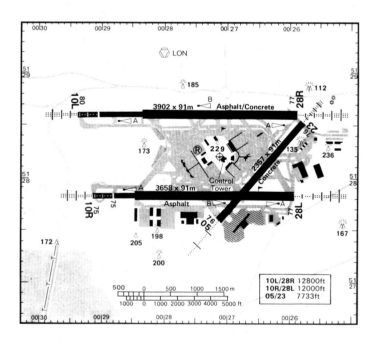

The earliest passenger reception facilities at Heathrow, in a tent. Richard Fairey's Great Western Aerodrome hanger.

attention of developers building satellite villages around the capital, though places such as Hayes, West Drayton, and Stanwell were expanded. An airfield at Hounslow Heath had seen the departure of the first commercial cross-Channel flight on 25 August 1919, and several other airfields were established near by. In 1929 Richard Fairey, who had made some of the most successful British planes to fight in the First World War, was asked to leave the premises the firm occupied at RAF Northolt. Faireys bought 150 acres of land between the Bath Road and the Great South West Road (which divided from the Bath Road at Cranford) and moved their test operations to this site, building a large hangar and laying down an exceptionally level stretch of grass. This new aerodrome was known by a variety of names, among them Heathrow.

During the early months of the Second World War it became apparent that there was a great need for a transport base close to London which could handle heavy aircraft. Heathrow was requisitioned in 1942 to remedy this deficiency, and in 1944 work began on the construction of the standard, triangular pattern of runways favoured in those days. However, the war ended before the completion of the airfield, and it was subsequently decided that the site should be adapted for civilian use. Ultimately it would become London's international airport, replacing Croydon and Northolt. Further runways were to put down in the shape of another triangle, the effect being of a Star of David. The advantage of this was that an aircraft could take off or land in any possible wind direction. Furthermore, since each runway was duplicated with a separation of some 4,500 feet, they could be used simultaneously.

History

The Great West Road, or Bath Road, was one of the most important stage-coach routes out of London. Travellers using it would have felt some trepidation as they left the outskirts of London, for the road crossed heathland which offered highwaymen perfect cover. Coachmen gave their horses some whip to speed them over this dangerous ground towards the safety of Slough.

Because of the nature of the ground it failed to attract the

Above: *Heathrow from the air: note the inner and outer taxiways (an unusual feature at a major airport) and the fuel farm in the*

foreground. Below: *the first scheduled flight from Heathrow: a BOAC Lancastrian leaves for its three-day 'Kangaroo' trip to Australia in 1946.* Bottom: *film editors at work aboard a BOAC Stratocruiser making the film of the Coronation ready for showing in New York.*

The first flight from the new airport took place on 1 January 1946, when a British South American Airways' Avro Lancastrian (a civil version of the Lancaster bomber) G-AGWG *Starlight* took off on a proving flight to Buenos Aires. Three months later a regular twice-weekly South American service was established and in May BOAC operated their first flight out of Heathrow – to Australia. The formal opening of the airport took place on 31 May 1946, but passengers enjoyed few facilities, being accommodated in marquees and old caravans sited on the north side. Soon after the official opening the first transatlantic flights arrived – Constellations of Pan-Am and American Overseas Airlines.

In the following year the three runways comprising the first triangle were completed and a start was made on those of the second triangle. Already the increasing use of aircraft commercially was giving rise to doubts that the facilities planned would be adequate. It was decided that in the long term the north-side terminal would prove impractical and so a tunnel was dug beneath Runway 1 to allow development in the central area. Later, expansion of this site led to the abandonment of Runways 3, 4 and 6.

Thus the central terminal buildings came into being. A new control tower formed the hub of the new work, with a 'short-haul' terminal (now Terminal 2) and an administration block (the Queens Building).

In 1954 RAF Northolt was closed to scheduled civil airline users (it had previously handled BEA services and those of several foreign operators) and overnight the traffic at Heathrow was more than doubled. Even with the new central terminal it was obvious that further expansion would be necessary, and in the late 1950s it was proposed that two new terminals should be built in the central area plus a cargo building. Because of the meteoric expansion of this side of the business, this last proposal was subsequently abandoned, with the Cargo Terminal eventually being placed on the south side of the airport: it was opened in December 1968.

These developments form the basis of the Heathrow we know today, yet a characteristic of airports is that they never exist in the same form for long, and the construction of a fourth terminal on the south side serves as an illustration of this.

Heathrow Today

Heathrow handles considerably more international passengers each year than any other airport in the world – more than 23,000,000 in 1982. Its total number of passengers (26,500,000) makes it the world's fourth busiest airport over all. More than 45,000 people are employed at Heathrow.

The advent of high-capacity, wide-bodied jet aircraft has changed the priorities of many facets of airport operation. The pressure is no longer on runways, for more passengers arrive and depart on fewer flights. There was a danger of congestion on the ground rather than in the air, as 500 or so passengers per aircraft were likely to use the facilities designed for half that number. Fortunately, enough warning was given of the arrival of the Jumbo on the scene for buildings to be enlarged and priorities changed. Terminal 3 can now handle 3,000 arriving passengers in an hour, with 2,800 departing. The increased loads being carried by short-haul aircraft have also brought about reappraisals of facilities at the terminals. It is primarily this factor which has made the building of a fourth terminal necessary.

From the passengers' point of view, the opening of the Heathrow rail link with the centre of London via the Piccadilly Line has been particularly welcome. Heathrow Station handles 24,000 passengers a day, moving walkways connecting the station with the three terminals.

Terminal 1

European and domestic flights into and out of Heathrow are handled by Terminal 1, together with flights to the Irish Republic and British Airways services to and from Miami and Chicago: these long-haul flights were moved to this terminal to make better use of facilities here that are quiet at certain times of day. About 11,000,000 passengers pass through this terminal each year; one of the features of its design is the method by which arriving and departing passengers are kept apart – arrivals use the ground floor and departures the upper one. The concept of the shuttle services (which ensure that passengers can get quickly to certain UK destinations without booking in advance) puts extra pressure on the terminal, as large waiting areas had to be incorporated into the domestic as well as the international piers. The Eurolounge, on the apron between Terminals 1 and 2 (and linked to both by moving walkways), provides further much-needed aircraft stands (five of them for wide-bodied jets) as well as a waiting area for 700 passengers.

Terminal 2

When first built in 1955 this was the first passenger building in the central area of the airport and dealt exclusively with the flights of BEA. Domestic flights were handled in an adjoining wing of the building which had its own access to aircraft. Terminal 2 (the Europa Building in those days) introduced the 'channel' system of flight handling in which passengers from up to ten flights could pass through controls separately, but at the same time.

When Terminal 1 was opened in 1968 the domestic, European, and Irish services were transferred there and the Europa Building became Terminal 2. In 1975 work began on a £20,000,000 scheme enlarging and modernising its facilities. This has resulted in a new, spacious ground-floor check-in concourse; new escalators, lifts and ramps between floors; and a new shopping complex, among other improvements. Dealing with short-haul flights to international destinations, Terminal 2 is able to handle 3,000 passengers per hour.

Terminal 3

Inter-continental passengers used the old Northside Terminal by the Bath Road until 1962 when the Oceanic Building was opened within the central area. At this time the Terminal's capacity was 2,400 passengers per hour, but the rapid growth of air traffic through the 1960s made these facilities inadequate, especially with the advent of Jumbos. Since Heathrow would be handling more of these high-capacity aircraft than any other European airport, the expansion of Terminal 3 was vital and in 1968 a start was made on a new programme of development. An area of thirty acres was concreted for parking stands for 747s. This was complemented by a new pier 915 feet long which led to ten gate-rooms, each capable of handling 500 passengers. A new arrivals

Above: *Concorde, capable of 1,400 mph, dawdling behind a tug at Heathrow.* Below: *fuel is all-important to airline economics. A 747 holds 39,000 gallons (177,294 litres) and a passenger of average weight 'consumes' his own weight in fuel every 1,500 miles on a fully-laden plane.*

Terminal 4

The new terminal is scheduled to come into operation in 1985, having cost £210,000,000 (this figure includes access roads and other facilities). It will help to increase the capacity of Heathrow from the present 27,000,000 to 38,000,000 passengers per year, and will allow the airport growth until the end of the present decade. The main difference between Terminal 4 and the existing terminals is that the new complex is designed to operate without piers. Its all-in-one airside concourse will contain bars, shops and four catering areas. The concourse will give direct access to sixteen wide-body aircraft stands, half of them capable of dealing with the stretched version of the 747. There will be complete separation of arriving and departing passengers which will be achieved by the use of different floor-levels. The throughput will be a maximum of 2,000 passengers an hour in each direction.

It is expected that several major operators, at present working from the central area, will be attracted to the new terminal which, it is hoped, will handle both European and long-haul flights.

Terminal 4 will be linked to the existing terminals by a new airside road and by the cargo tunnel. A looped extension of the Piccadilly Line will join it to London's Underground system.

Cargo Terminal

By value of goods handled, Heathrow can claim to be the foremost port in the UK: £16,000,000,000-worth of cargo passed through the airport in 1981. The terminal, situated on the south side of the airport, is linked to the central passenger area by a road tunnel used mainly by freight vehicles. Altogether there are twenty-six aircraft stands – six with facilities specially designed for the lofty holds of the freight version of the 747, and another six for the other, lower wide-bodies. The cargo area covers 160 acres and seventeen airlines lease bonded shed space from the BAA. There is another bonded site beyond the eastern perimeter of the airport, linked to the terminal by a secure road so that cargoes can be moved between the two sites under bond. There is also a spacious non-bonded warehouse area at the terminal. A hydrant system provides rapid refuelling and hence fast turn-round times. There is an animal quarantine station which includes an area for the RSPCA. Sophisticated X-Ray and decompression units are among the other facilities offered to freight customers.

It is always exhilarating to fly into London Heathrow. The sheer size of the field and density of air traffic requires the very best of controllers. Usually both runways are in use, with aircraft landing on 28L and departing from 28R. All relevant airfield details are to be found on Bovingdon VOR/ATIS 112.3. For STandard ARrivals the STAR chart indicates available routes inbound. From the north the radar controllers usually feed aircraft from Barkway VOR to Lambourne VOR, then in a westerly direction across the north of London, turning them in a lazy S-turn to roll out for an ILS approach on 28L. Owing to traffic density it is not unusual to be held in the stack as far back as Barkway VOR and then again at Lambourne VOR.

The approach to 28L lies over the south of the Thames past Westminster and Kew Gardens, with Richmond Park on the left. When fully established on the ILS, aircraft are handed over to the local controller for landing clearance.

After landing the commuter aircraft follow the greens on the inner or outer taxiways as directed by the ground controller to stands Bravo, Delta or November which are clustered round the central control tower.

Engine start clearance and departure information is obtained on 121.7, ATIS on 121.85, taxi information on 121.9, and line-up on 118.5. Aircraft on the SID for 28R fly with Windsor Castle to the left, beyond which are four mysterious green flashing lights at night – ghosts?

Top: *the Heathrow–Gatwick Airlink utilises a 28-seater Sikorsky S-61N*. Middle: *beyond the SAS DC 9 is the British Airways Tristar bay*. Below: *a tailpiece of liveries*.

terminal was added to the complex and the Oceanic Building converted into the long-haul departure terminal. Check-ins are situated on the ground floor where six island sites each provide twenty-four desks run by thirty-seven different airlines. Having checked in, escalators take passengers to the spacious departure lounge on the first floor, where there is also one of the largest duty-free shops in the world, as well as a buffet bar with seating for 500. Later developments have been an airside coach station which serves remote aircraft stands, and the improvement of Pier 7, the length of which was increased to more than 1,400 feet. At the same time its width was doubled to enable moving walkways to be installed, and these served seven new gateways. Pier 6 later received similar treatment.

Above: *specialist loading gear is necessary for this front-loading Pan-Am 747 freighter whereas (below) the DC 3 of Air Atlantique is loaded by more traditional methods. Right: coming (a British Midland DC 9) and going (Varig DC 10).*

LONDON
STANSTEAD

IATA Code: STN. **ICAO Code:** EGSS.

Elevation: 347 feet.

Site: 2.5 nm ENE of Bishop's Stortford. Close to M11.

Runway: 23/05. 3,048 metres (10,000 feet) × 61 metres (200 feet).

Apron:
Terminal area: eight aircraft up to B727/Trident size, or six B707 or two B747 plus four B707, etc.
Twelve parking stands away from terminal area.
The helicopter area is separate from fixed-wing parking areas.

Stansted Ground: 126.95 MHz.

Stansted Approach: 118.15; 125.55 MHz.

Traffic 1981–82
Terminal passengers: 300,200.
Commercial aircraft movements: 7,700.

Freight: 6,400 tonnes.

Spectator facilities: Open-air enclosure gives view of runway.

Stansted's wartime origins are well illustrated by this aerial view.

the Mediterranean. Tour operators remain the prime users of the airport, though its cargo facilities have been expanded (this being helped by the opening of the M11 motorway). Unusual traffic from Stansted is the shipment of valuable horses from the stables and studs at Newmarket to all parts of the world. A handful of scheduled flights operate from Stansted, mainly to Europe (those to Amsterdam and Brussels being particularly popular), and there is also a thriving aircraft maintenance business here. It is the home base for the Civil Aviation Authority Flying Unit, which is responsible for inspecting lighting and landing-aids at airports which come under its control.

World attention was concentrated on Stansted in February 1982, when an Air Tanzania Boeing 737 landed here after being hijacked during an internal flight in its home country. It also visited Nairobi, Jeddah and Athens for refuelling. Stansted was closed for twenty-six hours while negotiations with the terrorists took place. These ended with the peaceful release of the hostages and the arrest of the hijackers.

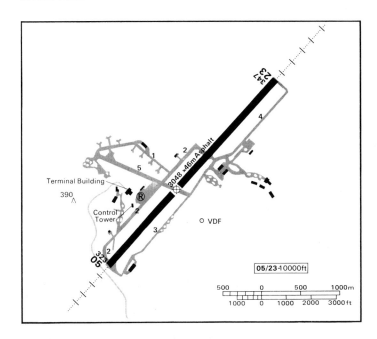

Quite frequently, the weather is acceptable at Stansted when meteorological conditions are bad at Heathrow or Gatwick. If weather is marginal one monitors regional trends on London Volmet (South). Stansted is well equipped to cope with aircraft diverted from the other London airports. Its radar will feed incoming aircraft on to the ILS for Runway 23 and, after landing, aircraft are directed to the right on to the large aprons to the west of the airfield.

The proximity of the M11 makes the airport ideally suited to handle road freight traffic round the clock. In particular there is a growing use of Stansted for night mail services. The mail-sacks are loaded from GPO vans using conveyor belts. The handlers insist that music from the on-board tape recorder helps them to load fast and easily! This is useful as there is a hefty penalty clause for late arrival of mail at destination.

As all departures must be co-ordinated by London, departure clearance should be requested early. The SID is extremely complicated and, to their credit, London try to ease the pain by simplifying routing when outbound aircraft pass under their control.

At the time of writing a marathon Board of Enquiry is still sitting to determine the fate of Stansted, the third of the trio of BAA airports serving the capital. The BAA would like to expand Stansted to relieve pressure on Heathrow and Gatwick. There is strong local opposition to this.

Stansted was built as a USAF bomber station in 1942. After the war civilian cargo airliners (converted Halifax bombers and the ubiquitous DC3) shared its facilities with the USAF. In 1948 it was first suggested that Stansted could be London's second airport but Gatwick was chosen instead. Soon afterwards Stansted was enlarged by the Americans, the main runway being extended to 10,000 feet so that it might be used for their long-range jet bombers.

The USAF withdrew from Stansted in 1957, but it was subsequently used by Transport Command for trooping flights and by civilian charter tour operators flying to Scandinavia and

Above: *Stansted has comprehensive engineering facilities: here an American 727 is being refurbished.* Below: *the immaculate aircraft of small overseas airlines are exotic visitors to Stansted.* Right: *a Boeing 747–249F of the freight carrier, Flying Tigers, being unloaded at Stansted.*

LUTON

IATA Code: LTN. **ICAO Code:** EGGW.

Area: 676 acres.

Elevation: 526 feet.

Site: 1.5 nm E of Luton.

Runways: 08/26.   2,160 × 46 metres (7,087 × 150 feet) – asphalt with porous friction course – LCG II.
There are two grass runways, 793 metres and 395 metres, to the north of the main runway.

Apron: Seventeen stands. Concrete and asphalt.

Luton Ground: 121.75 MHz.

Luton Tower: 120.2 MHz.

Luton Approach: 129.55; 128.75; 127.3 MHz.

Traffic 1981–82
Terminal passengers: 1,979,707.
Passenger movements: 17,703.
Commercial movements: 35,068.

Freight: 13,981 tonnes.

Spectator facilities: By taxiway with good view of runway.

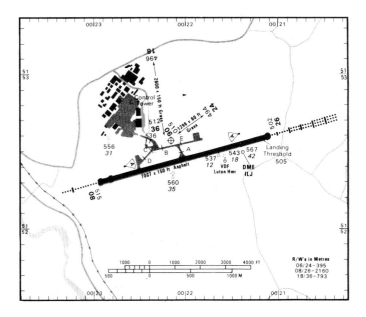

The Control Tower at Luton.

History

Of the four airports that claim to serve the London region, Luton is the only one to be operated independently of the British Airports Authority. In fact it is one of the most successful of Britain's municipal airports, unique in being only two miles from the town centre. It proudly boasts that it is 'Britain's Premier Holiday Airport'.

Its story began fifty years ago when Luton Town Council adopted a proposal that an airport should be built to become '. . . London's Terminal Airport on its northern boundary'. The site chosen was Buttermilk Hill, which overlooks Luton from the south-east. Although the top of the hill was a reasonably level plateau, 50,000 cubic yards of soil still had to be pulled up the hill to make the surface even enough for a first-class airfield. On 16 July 1938 a great air pageant was staged to mark the opening of the airfield, over a hundred aircraft taking part. Some of these roared overhead 'at terrifying speeds of over 200 mph', while the climax of the show was the 'suicide leaps' of the Viennese parachutist Carl Siemendl, who jumped off the wing of a Tiger Moth flying at a height of only 150 feet. On his second jump the parachute tore and he was lucky to escape serious injury.

By this time Luton was a thriving industrial community. Vauxhall Motors had become one of the giants of the British motor manufacturers having moved to Luton from London in 1905. The Percival Aircraft Company had established their factory by the newly born airfield in 1936. They made the famous Gull monoplane – an outstanding light aircraft that took first and second places in the King's Cup air race in 1938.

The outbreak of war in 1939 brought further aviation-based industries to Luton, including the aero-engine manufacturer, D. Napier & Son. The airfield was taken over by the War Ministry and this effectively put an end to its commercial development until many years later. However many interesting technological developments first saw the light of day at Luton. The famous 'Flying Bedstead' – the forerunner of the Harrier jump-jet – performed its first vertical take-off trials here, and a Canberra bomber, with a Napier rocket engine fixed on improvised mountings in its bomb-bay, reached a height of 70,310 feet on a trip which began and ended at Luton. When the Canberra reached its normal ceiling of 40,000 feet the pilot ignited the rocket engine and began his prayers while he made a more or less uncontrolled ascent into the stratosphere. The descent must have been even more unnerving with the plane plummeting back to earth out of control until a normal atmosphere began to give the controls 'bite' and allowed the pilot to exercise his normal skills.

The far-sightedness of Luton Town Council was displayed again in 1959 when they decided to build a concrete runway 5,432 feet (1,699 metres) long. Their faith in the potential of the continental holiday trade was the foundation of the airport's success in later years. In 1960 just 4,000 passengers used Luton: two years later this figure had increased to 43,000, while in 1963 (when the runway was extended by another 1,200 feet) the number had risen to 137,000. By the end of the 1960s nearly 2,000,000 passengers a year were using the facilities provided at Luton and the new terminal building opened in 1966 was already hard-pressed. The situation grew even worse in the 1970s when the magic 3,000,000 mark was passed.

Unfortunately, at this time the Government were supporting the idea of a third London Airport to be built on Maplin Sands, and their intention was to close Luton completely when the new airport was ready to operate in 1980. Thus they refused to consent to further building at Luton, and the management were forced to use a huge marquee as an arrival hall. Although this improvisation worked it was hardly helpful to the efforts aimed at establishing Luton as a major international airport!

The 1978 Government White Paper on Airports Policy abandoned Maplin and allowed for the growth of Luton, placing the maximum capacity of its single terminal at 5,000,000 passengers a year. In 1981–82 the airport was used by 1,979,707 passengers, a 5.1 per cent decrease over the level of the previous year, reflecting the onset of depressed economic conditions. Nevertheless the major reconstruction of the terminal facilities continued. The first phase of the redevelopment plan was completed early in 1981, while the succeeding two phases are scheduled for completion in 1984. The total cost will exceed £8,000,000 and the improvements will help to confirm Luton's status as a London Area Category A Gateway Airport, handling up to 3,500,000 passengers each year efficiently and comfortably.

Traffic

Luton is Britain's fifth busiest airport (after Heathrow, Gatwick, Manchester and Glasgow). As we have seen, its business comes mainly from the holiday sector of the market, two of the largest operators in this field, Britannia and Monarch, being based at Luton. There are a number of reasons why these companies find Luton so attractive.

Its facilities are tailored for this traffic. It has its own independent Air Traffic Control which keeps delays to a minimum and thus saves on fuel costs. This Control has all the latest sophisticated aids, including secondary surveillance radar – the first British airport after Heathrow to install this system. Baggage handling is rapid at Luton because aircraft are close to the terminal building.

There is parking for more than 10,000 cars *at the airport*.

In terms of travelling time, Luton is the closest airport to the centre of London (journey time from Luton to St Pancras is now down to twenty-eight minutes). Access from the M1 is easy.

Airlines are able to make additional revenue from in-flight duty-free sales since it is Council policy that there should be no duty-free shop at Luton. This concession to operators is valuable and offsets other costs which might be marginally higher at Luton than elsewhere.

The safety facilities at Luton are among the best to be found in Britain. Fire-fighting equipment includes two of the latest Javelin tenders, each carrying 10,000 litres of water and 1,200 litres of liquid foam. There is also a Carmichael Rapid Intervention unit.

In adverse weather conditions there is a fleet of thirteen vehicles to combat the effects of snow on the runway, while a new Rolba Urea Spreader can keep it free of ice.

Unique Flexibuses are available to take passengers to and from their aircraft. These vehicles are one and a half times the length of ordinary coaches and are jointed in the middle to make them manœuvrable. Up to 130 passengers with their hand baggage can be carried in a Flexibus.

Resident Airlines

Britannia Airways have been operating out of Luton for more

A Britannia Airways Boeing 737-200 loading an Inclusive Tour flight at Luton.

A Bandeirante of Datapost at Luton. Painted in Post Office red it is one of a fleet of seven aircraft which provide an express parcels and packages service to all parts of Britain. Luton is one of the bases for this service.

than twenty-two years. A part of the Thomson organisation since 1965, they are Britain's second largest airline after British Airways in terms of the number of passengers carried. Britannia have one of the largest fleets of Boeing 737s in Europe and are planning to use the new 767 when it becomes available in 1984. This revolutionary airliner, built for economy, will seat 269 passengers – twice the number of a 737. Besides being carrier for Thomson Holidays, Britannia's aircraft are also chartered by other tour operators – in fact half of their business comes from outside the parent company. They maintain extensive engineering and training facilities at Luton.

Monarch are also based at Luton and are a part of the Cosmos holiday group. They operate 737s and 757s, the latter being powered by Rolls-Royce RB 211 535 engines. They, too, serve other tour operators as well as Cosmos – notably Ellermans', Pegasus and Horizon.

McAlpine Aviation are Europe's largest business aircraft charter company, benefiting from the needs of oil companies to have their executives rushed from one remote location to another. They operate eighteen Hawker Siddeley 125 executive jets, plus two of the Series 700 which have transatlantic capability. In addition McAlpine own five other types of aircraft so that they can almost certainly offer a potential customer the aircraft best suited to his needs.

Visually, Luton airport runway protrudes to the east of the town like the base of the letter Q. Arrivals from London Control on a radar-to-radar handover are usually cleared to the NDB 'LUT', thence to the ILS on Runway 26. As there is only this one runway it is important for inbound pilots to receive up-to-the-minute weather information, particularly wind velocity. Volmet London (South) 128.6 regularly transmits weather information for all major airports in the region including suitable diversions. If the visibility is poor, say less than 1,100 metres, the Runway Visual Range (RVR) is passed to inbound aircraft. This provides a pilot with the visibility he can expect from the cockpit during an approach in poor weather. It is calculated for touchdown, midway, and far end of the runway.

After landing, the aircraft is taxied to the north of the airfield to the aprons. The controllers have to be very slick to deal with the rapid turnround of the typical Inclusive Tour (IT) operators.

The usual IT departure, from either runway direction, is to the south initially; thence to the south-east and the sun.

MANCHESTER

IATA Code: MAN. **ICAO Code:** EGCO.

Area: 1,042 acres.

Elevation: 256 feet.

Site: 7.5 nm SW of city.

Runway: 06/24. 3,048 × 46 metres (10,000 × 150 feet), plus 23-metre hard shoulder. Asphalt with friction course. Arrester bed at western end.

Landing category ICAO: Category III (b).

Apron: Thirty-seven stands: ten can accommodate wide-bodied aircraft (four with double overbridge unloading). Accommodation for an additional three 747s and one B727 to be available in 1984.

Manchester Tower: 118.7 MHz.

Manchester Approach: 119.4 MHz.

Traffic 1981
Terminal passengers: 4,720,000.
Commercial movements: 58,457

Freight: 32,535 tonnes.

Spectator facilities: Access is allowed to terraces and piers above the Terminal Building at a small charge (tokens purchased at entrances).

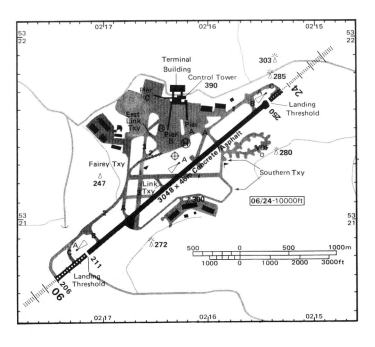

History
Manchester showed an unmatched zest for flying from the earliest days of aviation. After all, it was a Mancunian pair – John Alcock and Arthur Whitten-Brown – who had managed the first non-stop crossing of the Atlantic in 1919. Even before this Manchester was to the forefront, being the finishing-point of the *Daily Mail* Air Race of 1910. The earliest scheduled flights from Manchester also began in 1919: the Avro Civil Aviation Service started operations between the city, Southport, and Blackpool. Altogether 194 flights were completed without mishap. In 1922 Daimler Airways began a service to Croydon using De Havilland

An airport takes on an added glamour at night.

34s, but a fatal accident on 14 September 1923 ended this enterprise. These operations all worked out of the old military airfield at Alexandra Park, which finally closed in 1924. The far-sighted Manchester City Corporation sponsored a new airfield at Barton which opened on the first day of 1930. This aerodrome soon proved to be too small for the larger commercial aircraft then coming into use, and so in 1935 a start was made on a new airport at Ringway which was officially opened on 25 June 1938. It claimed to be Britain's first municipally-owned civil airport (opening just a month before Luton) and certainly the facilities it offered put it among the leading airports of the day, even though its airstrip was of grass.

Although Ringway was not taken over by the military during the war, it served a useful function being a leading centre for parachute training. Its No. 1 Parachute School trained 60,000 men, who made a total of some 400,000 descents. To facilitate this three concrete runways were constructed, the longest (06/24) being the basis for the one used today.

After the end of the war civilian services resumed with the operation of an Air France service to Paris in June 1946. In the following month a route was opened between Croydon, Manchester and Belfast using an Avro XIX. The first transatlantic service from Manchester Ringway (as it was still called) was flown by Sabena in 1953.

Modern Manchester
In 1962 a new terminal was opened which was capable of taking 3,000,000 passengers per year. It was soon apparent, however, that Manchester's new status as Britain's third airport would entail catering for 5,000,000 passengers. This early appreciation of the growth pattern of air transport meant that Manchester

Nearly 120 tons of Jumbo crossing the tunnel at Manchester.

Opposite page, above: *early days at Ringway: passengers disembark from a Dragon Rapide*. Below: *wartime at Ringway*. This page: *aerial view of Manchester International showing the extended runway*.

kept ahead in the boom years of the 1970s, and earned its reputation for being a comfortable airport, seldom suffering from the chaos of overcrowding that afflicted its rivals at this time.

Its major development of recent years has undoubtedly been the lengthening of the runway to 10,000 feet, which enables a wide-bodied aircraft to operate with 100 extra passengers, or with an increased range of 500 miles. Since these improvements were carried out mainly at night, and the normal operations of the airport were carried on almost without interruption, this major constructional work was a triumph both for the contractors and for the airport itself. The first phase of the scheme was to bring the existing runway up to ultimate modern standards by strengthening, reprofiling, and widening it. A new fast turn-off taxiway was added and a full Category III (b) lighting system installed (this is monitored by a computer which is able to detect a single lamp failure on any one of the twenty-eight circuits). A deep new asphalt surface was put down with friction course to give maximum adhesion in the wet.

In March 1981 work began on the western runway extension. To add 800 feet to the total length of the runway involved major earthmoving works. The River Bollin had to be diverted and its valley filled in – without spoiling its natural beauty. About 450,000 tonnes of stone were brought from Derbyshire to achieve this – a wagon-load every three minutes. Amazingly the £8,600,000 contract was completed four months ahead of schedule. It included a sophisticated arrester bed at the end of the extension which is filled with sintered ash pellets and should stop a 747 at fifty knots within sixty metres (the over-all length of the arrester is ninety metres). Beyond the arrester is a steep slope down to the River Bollin in its new valley.

As has been remarked before, a characteristic of a successful airport is its continuously changing features. Although the runway extension has been the major undertaking recently, significant changes and expansion have taken place within the terminal itself. A new-look international departure lounge with a duty-free shop reminiscent of the most plush West End store has been opened, while the famous concourse has received a face-lift. The 'market place' look of the refreshment area is a pioneering concept in airport catering: colourful, exciting and deservedly popular with passengers. However, the most significant of recent plans is the decision to give priority to the building of a separate domestic module which will relieve the increasing pressure on the present terminal facilities prior to the building of a second passenger terminal in 1990.

It may not be widely known that Manchester supports night newspaper freight operations. Typically the empty freighter aircraft arrives at night on a radar-to-radar handover and flies an ILS to Runway 06. Even in the early hours, the airport is wide awake and bustling, with the apron brightly lit. This arrival is in good time to refuel and take the newspapers on board via mobile conveyor belts. Taxiing and take-off are usually speedily executed as there are fewer movements at night.

Aircraft leave controlled airspace on the SID. One unique aspect of night flying is that there is no solar heating to energise the lower layers of air near the surface of the earth. Thus there can be relatively very strong winds at low levels unimpeded by surface turbulence. Accurate assessment of drift makes for adherence to the SID. At Manchester the requirement is to avoid flying over built-up areas; noise abatement is better if aircraft can fly the SID accurately.

Above: *the Aero Spacelines 'Guppy', converted from the old Stratocruiser, is a frequent visitor to Manchester. It is used to convey completed wing sections for Airbus manufacture.* Below: *artist's impression of the new duty-free shopping area at Manchester International.* Right: *the concourse is a famous example of period architecture.*

PRESTWICK

IATA Code: PIK. **ICAO Code:** EGPK.

Area: 1,742 acres.

Elevation: 64 feet.

Site: 1 nm NE of Prestwick.

Runways: 13/31. 3,139 × 46 metres (10,300 × 150 feet) – concrete/asphalt.
03/21. 1,829 × 61 metres (6,000 × 200 feet).

Apron: Stands for eight aircraft.

Prestwick Ground: 118.15 MHz.

Prestwick Approach: 120.55 MHz.

Traffic 1981–82
Terminal passengers: 253,400.
Commercial movements: 4,400.

Freight: 16,000 tonnes.

Spectator facilities: On roof of Terminal.

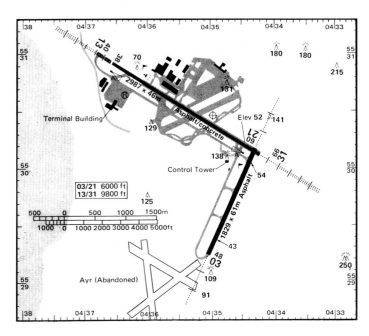

The great length of the runway at Prestwick unfortunately belies the importance of the airport.

was the only European airport open to traffic. Between October 1976 and September 1978 there were just three hours when conditions at Prestwick fell within Category III (a) – Cloudbase 0–100 feet; Visibility 200–400 metres – and seven hours when they were within Category II – Cloudbase 100–200 feet; Visibility 400–800 metres. During the remaining 17,510 hours the meteorological conditions exceeded this.

Prestwick Airport originated as a grass airfield serving as a flying school run by the Duke of Hamilton and Group Captain D. F. McIntyre, the two men who had won fame as being the first to fly over Everest in 1933. The company that they founded (which prospered up to the outbreak of war) was named Scottish Aviation, and undertook air charter work and aircraft repairs as well as the training of pilots. The RAF took over Prestwick at the beginning of the Second World War and used it as a training station. Its useful situation was demonstrated by a pilot ferrying new American bombers across the Atlantic. Separated from his formation, he overshot Aldergrove (Belfast) airfield and landed at Prestwick, to the surprise of station personnel. He had flown from Gandar in Newfoundland. The first concrete runway, measuring 6,600 by 300 feet, was put down in 1941. Its width was

A battered photograph from the archives shows the famous Orangefield Hotel and a BOAC Stratocruiser.

The present status of Prestwick must be something of a disappointment to the BAA who took over the airport in 1966. It must be the most under-used intercontinental airport in Europe: the Winter 1983 timetable shows only seven incoming transatlantic flights scheduled per week, and only two operators using it – North-West Orient and Air Canada. Of course, business improves in the summer, but there is no denying that Prestwick is declining, with only 253,400 passengers using the airport in 1981–82 compared with 650,000 in 1976–77.

However, there are some advantages enjoyed by Prestwick which are denied to other, busier, airports. The local climate is particularly favourable for flying, and this was one of the main reasons why the first (grass) airfield was established here in 1935. Thus Prestwick has often been used as a diversionary airport when other UK destinations have been fogbound. The ever-increasing sophistication of blind-flying aids has led to fewer flights being diverted there, but it remains an important function of the airport. In the 1960s there were occasions when Prestwick

exceptional, but cross-winds on this stretch of coast are often severe, and pilots were frequently very tired when they arrived and their landings could be erratic. A year later a second runway, 4,500 feet long, was constructed. Prestwick became one of the main destinations for brand-new bombers from factories in America.

The pilots then would have welcomed the sight of the Orangefield Hotel, which was used as a terminal building. This had once been an old manor house, known to Robert Burns. Over the original doorway were carved his words: 'A pleasant spot near sandy wilds.' The roof of the hotel was modified to support the control tower. This distinctive building was demolished to make way for the present terminal.

When the BAA took over Prestwick in 1966 it was a reasonably busy airport with excellent modern facilities. The main runway had been extended to 9,800 feet (there are overruns at each end to give an effective length of 10,000 feet). A new control tower was built at the intersection of the two runways. The terminal had comprehensive international facilities which were seldom overcrowded. Prestwick had been designated as Britain's second transcontinental airport, and a major part of its business came from charter operators offering tours of the Highlands. However its rather remote situation was a disadvantage, as was the lack of flights to onward destinations. Thus business at Prestwick has declined, operators preferring to fly into places where onward routings are comprehensive and access to the motorway network is immediate. Nevertheless, Prestwick has other functions in aviation (freight-handling, flight-training, maintenance, etc.) and the Scottish Tourist Board as well as the BAA are always quick to confirm the airport's importance.

Top left: *the spacious concourse at Prestwick on a busy day.* Right: *North-West Orient are a loyal user of Prestwick for transatlantic flights.* Above: *life at Prestwick was at its most hectic during the Second World War when it was a receiving base for American bombers to be used in Europe.*

The weather factor at Prestwick is remarkably good all the year round, and this makes the airfield especially suitable for diversions caused by bad met conditions elsewhere. Prestwick ATC is geared to helping incoming aircraft which may be running low on fuel and anxious to land as soon as possible. Their weather is continuously broadcast on Volmet North to enable pilots to keep up to date with trends.

Assuming the weather is within limits for making an approach, the Radar Controller will feed the inbound aircraft to NDB PE co-located with the outer marker for an ILS to Runway 31.

First impressions here are of an enormously long runway 31/13, a welcome sight indeed to transatlantic and diversion traffic. The hard standings are spacious and equipped to deal with the very largest wide-bodied passenger aircraft. All facilities are available for en-route planning and departures are usually effected easily and quickly.